A Teacher's Guide to Classroom Research

A Teacher's Guide to Classroom Research

SECOND EDITION

David Hopkins

Open University Press
BUCKINGHAM · PHILADELPHIA

Open University Press
Celtic Court
22 Ballmoor
Buckingham
MK18 1XW

and 1900 Frost Road, Suite 101
Bristol, PA 19007, USA

First edition published 1985, reprinted 1987, 1988,
1990, 1992

First published in this second edition 1993

Reprinted in this edition 1994, 1995

A catalogue record of this book is available from the
British Library

ISBN 0 335 19065 0 (pb)

Library of Congress Cataloging-in-Publication Data
Hopkins, David 1949–
    A teacher's guide to classroom research / David
Hopkins. – 2nd ed.
            p.   cm.
    Includes bibliographical references (p.   ) and
    indexes.
    ISBN 0–335–19065–0
    1. Action research in education.   2. Classroom
management–Research.   3. Observation
(Educational method)   4. Curriculum
change.   I. Title.
LB1028.24.H67   1993   93–16193
370'.78–dc20   CIP

Typeset by Type Study, Scarborough
Printed in Great Britain by St Edmundsbury Press Ltd,
Bury St Edmunds, Suffolk

For

Jeroen, Jessica and Dylan

with love

In short the outstanding characteristic of the extended professional (teacher) is a capacity for autonomous professional self development through systematic self study, through the study of the work of other teachers and through the testing of ideas by classroom research procedures.

Lawrence Stenhouse
An Introduction to Curriculum Research and Development

Appreciating a phenomenon is a fateful decision, for it eventually entails a commitment – to the phenomenon and to those exemplifying it – to render it with fidelity and without violating its integrity. Entering the world of the phenomenon is a radical and drastic method of appreciation.

David Matza
Becoming Deviant

And what is good, Phaedrus,
And what is not good –
Need we ask anyone to tell us these things?

Robert Pirsig
Zen and the Art of Motorcycle Maintenance

▷ Contents

▷ Acknowledgements

I am grateful to the late Mike Bruce, Don Cochrane, Peter Norman, Jean Rudduck and especially Ann Kilcher for the care with which they reviewed the original manuscript; and for conversations that clarified my thinking on this and other matters. Their friendship and professional collaboration have meant a great deal to me. Suzzane de Castell, Gill Harper-Jones, Pat Holborn, my sister Mary Schofield, Louise Pelletier and David Pritchard also provided material and intellectual support at critical and opportune times: my thanks to them too. A number of colleagues and students graciously allowed me to use some of their material as illustrations and examples in the first edition. In this regard, I am indebted to Stan Auerbach, Judy Byer, Heather Lockhard, Sandra Meister, Marianne Schmidt, Ann Waldo and Harvey Walker. The three anonymous reviewers of the original book proposal made comments that encouraged me to revise and improve that manuscript. I anticipate that at least two of them were satisfied with the outcome.

In preparing the second edition of this book, my colleagues at Cambridge have been characteristically generous in taking time to review and help me with the manuscript. I am particularly grateful to Mel Ainscow for his thoughtful and creative comments, and more generally for exploring with me the boundaries of professional partnership. Colin

Conner, Dave Ebbutt and Julie Howard also reviewed parts of the manuscript and made helpful comments. I am grateful to the Bedfordshire LEA/University of Cambridge Institute of Education 'Developing Successful Learning Project', Howard Bradley and Rob Bollington, Jere Brophy and Tom Good, Walter Doyle, Rex Gibson, David Hargreaves, Pamela Hughes, David Jeffries, Denis Lawton, James McKernan and The Sanders Draper School for letting me use some of their material in this new edition. John Skelton, my publisher at the Open University Press, has been most supportive throughout the production of both editions.

The argument of the book was developed from ideas originally published in the *CARN Bulletin*, the DES booklet *Planning for School Development*, the *Empowered School, Managing Schools Today, Phi Delta Kappan, School Organization* and *The Times Educational Supplement*. Finally, I must also acknowledge the Deakin University Press, the Ford Teaching Project and Universitetsforlaget AS for allowing me to reproduce copyright material.

As always it was Marloes Hopkins de Groot who provided the shelter conditions under which the work could take place: thanks to her for this and many other things.

▷ Preface to the Second Edition

The educational landscape in Britain and most other Western countries has changed dramatically since this book was originally published in 1985. The increase in centralized policy making, however, far from undermining the role of 'teacher researcher', has in my opinion made such a professional ethic all the more necessary. It is becoming increasingly obvious that 'top-down' change does not 'mandate what matters', and that it is local implementation, the work of teachers, that determines student outcomes. If we are serious about enhancing the quality of education in our schools, teachers need to be more, not less, involved in curriculum development and evaluation.

It seems to me that the major difference between now and the mid-1980s is that teacher researchers have increasingly to take a whole school perspective. They now have to interpret and adapt policy to their own teaching situation and to link their classroom research work to that of other colleagues and whole-school priorities.

In preparing this second edition of *A Teacher's Guide to Classroom Research*, I have tried to take this new perspective into account while retaining the structure and simplicity of the original book. In particular, I have emphasized the crucial role of classroom observation in supporting teacher and school development, added a new chapter on linking classroom research to other whole school initiatives, updated the text in light of the changing context, and taken the opportunity to rewrite where I had originally been too bland, confused or just got it wrong. There has also been a burgeoning literature on classroom or action research since this book was first published, and I have referenced much of that too.

As I note in Chapter 1, all books, even primers on classroom research, are in some sense biographical. In so far as my views have changed or evolved over the past years, they are also reflected in the rewriting. I note some of these professional influences in Chapter 1, but it was also during this period that our children were born. The combination of new professional and intense personal experiences has resulted, I think, in a more holistic and practical approach to education, schooling and hopefully my own life. More specifically in terms of this book, the experiences of the past few years, besides broadening my view of teacher research into a whole school context, have made me increasingly frustrated with 'strategies' that are insufficiently practical, are not related to the daily reality of classrooms and school life, and only have tenuous links with student experience and achievement.

The book continues to have a modest aim: it is to provide teachers and students with a practical guide to doing research in their own classrooms and to linking these research efforts to whole school developments. Despite the proliferation of texts on action research in recent years, I believe that there is still a place for a practical and straightforward introduction to teacher-based classroom research; particularly one that is committed to teacher and school development. In this way, the book complements the existing literature rather than competes with it.

In re-reading the book I was struck by how far the original text was influenced by the work of Lawrence Stenhouse and how relevant his ideas still are for us today. In the educational crisis that we are currently experiencing, we need more people of his stature who have a vision of education and can translate it into a coherent philosophy and a pragmatic course of action. On my office wall there is a quotation from Stenhouse that is on his memorial plaque in the grounds of the University of East Anglia:

> It is teachers who, in the end, will change the world of the school by understanding it.

I hope that in some small way this book will contribute to that aspiration.

▷ **CHAPTER 1**

A Teacher's Guide to
Classroom Research

This is a practical guide for teachers who wish to undertake research in their classrooms and schools for the purpose of improving practice. Classroom research, in the sense that I refer to it here, is an act undertaken by teachers, to enhance their own or a colleague's teaching, to test the assumptions of educational theory in practice, or as a means of evaluating and implementing whole school priorities. So when I write of classroom research or of the teacher as researcher, I am not envisioning scores of teachers assuming a research role and carrying out research projects to the exclusion of their teaching. My vision is of teachers who have extended their role to include critical reflection upon their craft with the aim of improving it.

Although lip service is often paid to this idea, we live in an educational system that tends to limit individual initiative by encouraging conformity and control. Teachers and pupils (and society too) deserve better than that. Undertaking research in their own and colleagues' classrooms is one way in which teachers can take increased responsibility for their actions and create a more energetic and dynamic environment in which teaching and learning can occur.

The origins of teacher research as a movement can be traced back to the Schools Council's Humanities Curriculum Project (HCP) (1967–72) with its emphasis on an experimental curriculum and the reconceptualization of curriculum development as curriculum research. HCP, in its attempt to encourage a non-partisan and critically reflective attitude to teaching on the part of teachers, had a radical and controversial influence on teaching in British schools during the 1970s.

Following HCP, the concept of teacher research was nurtured by John Elliott and Clem Adelman in the Ford Teaching Project (1972–75). The project involved 40 primary and secondary school teachers in examining their classroom practice through action research. These teachers developed hypotheses about their teaching which could be shared with other teachers and used to enhance their own teaching.

At about the same time, Lawrence Stenhouse, who directed the Humanities Curriculum Project, further popularized the concept of 'the teacher as researcher' by utilizing it as the major theme in his influential book, *An Introduction to Curriculum Research and Development* (Stenhouse 1975). Encouraged by the considerable impact that Stenhouse had on the theory and practice of curriculum and teaching, and the popularity and publicity enjoyed by the Ford Teaching Project, the teacher research movement has mushroomed. As well as burgeoning teacher research groups in the UK, Australia, the USA and Canada, there are pockets of teacher-researchers in Scandinavia, France, Chile and elsewhere. Although teacher research was not an entirely new concept in the late 1960s, it is from this period that it became an identifiable movement.

Much, however, has changed in the context of education in most Western countries since the concept of the teacher as researcher became popular. The main difference between the 1970s and the 1990s is that classroom research has increasingly to be seen within a whole school context. It is no longer sufficient for teachers to do research in their own classrooms, without relating their enquiries to the work of their colleagues and the aims and direction of the school as a whole. We need to strive consciously for a synthesis between teacher research and school development. That is why this book is not just a primer on classroom research techniques, but also attempts to relate teacher research to whole school improvement efforts.

All books emerge out of a specific set of individual circumstances that have influenced the author, and this book is no exception. The journey that preceded this book is still continuing, and so the story remains unfinished. But two influences in particular have been crucial in developing the ideas presented here and provide a context in which to consider the book. The first is the work of Lawrence Stenhouse. In the Humanities Curriculum Project and his other work, Stenhouse was primarily concerned with the concept of emancipation. He wrote (1983: 163):

> My theme is an old-fashioned one – emancipation . . .
> The essence of emancipation as I conceive it is the intellectual, moral and spiritual autonomy which we recognise when we eschew paternalism and the role of authority and hold ourselves obliged to appeal to judgement.

There are three levels at which this concept of emancipation can operate – at the level of the student, the teacher and the school.

At the level of the student, emancipation refers to the ability to stand outside the teacher's authority on forms of knowledge, and to discover and own it for oneself. It was in the Humanities Curriculum Project that Stenhouse most notoriously signalled for his commitment to this theme. In that project he was principally concerned with the emancipation of pupils through a particular teaching strategy. There were three elements to this aspect of the project: the use of discussion, the use of documents as evidence to inform discussion, and the assumption by the teacher of the role of neutral chairperson. By adopting this approach,

Stenhouse was moving away from a teacher-dominated classroom to a setting where pupils, unconstrained by the authority of the teacher, could create meaning for themselves on the basis of evidence and discussion.

If HCP was in part a curriculum designed to emancipate pupils, the phrase 'teacher as researcher' was intended to do the same for teachers. Teachers are too often the servants of heads, advisers, researchers, textbooks, curriculum developers, examination boards or the Department for Education among others. By adopting a research stance, teachers are liberating themselves from the control position they so often find themselves in. Stenhouse encouraged teachers to follow the specification of a curriculum or teaching strategy, but at the same time to assess it critically. Such curriculum proposals and teaching specifications are probably intelligent but not necessarily correct, and their effectiveness should therefore be monitored by teachers in the classroom. By adopting this critical approach, by taking a research stance, the teacher is engaged not only in a meaningful professional development activity, but also engaged in a process of refining, and becoming more autonomous in, professional judgement. This applies as much to the National Curriculum as it did to the HCP.

The third level at which emancipation can operate is that of the school. Here it is a question of the school liberating itself from a bureaucratic and control-oriented educational system. The image of the 'ideal' type of emancipated school is represented by the words 'autonomous', 'creative', 'moving' or 'problem-solving'. These successful schools take the opportunity of the recent changes and use them to support developments already underway or planned for in the school. They adapt external change for internal purposes. In the most successful or emancipated schools, there is also a realization that successful change involves learning on the part of teachers. This implies that successful change strategies involve a seamless web of activities that focus on, are integrated with and enhance the daily work of teachers. This can result in quite profound alterations to the culture of the school and the ways in which teachers, heads and governors work together towards the goal of student achievement.

The second influence on this book is more personal. During the 1970s, I trained as a teacher and taught, worked as an Outward Bound instructor and mountain guide, and read for postgraduate degrees in education. Although somewhat different activities, they were all characterized by a desire, often hesitant and naive, to create ways in which people could take more control of their own lives. Irrespective of the context – practice teaching, an 'O' level history class, counselling a 'delinquent' pupil, assisting in a youth club, on the rock face, out in the wilderness, or discussing ideas in a seminar – there were similarities in overall aim and pedagogic structure.

Later, as a teacher in a Canadian university, I taught courses in curriculum development, analysis of teaching, classroom research, and found in Stenhouse's work a theoretical framework within which I could put my ideas into action. The book emerged from that experience, more specifically from a course I taught in classroom research and some papers I wrote on the topic (Hopkins 1982, 1984a, b). Thus, the book is based on a set of ideas that have the enhancement of teacher judgement and autonomy as a specific goal, and is grounded within the practical realities of teachers and students.

This interest in classroom-based work, although always in my mind linked to school improvement, has assumed a broader perspective since coming to Cambridge. Much of my work over the past seven years or so at the Institute of Education, has been concerned with assisting teachers, schools and local education authorities (LEAs) to handle and reflect on the change process. I have learned an enormous amount from them, as I have from my involvement in the evaluation of TVEI, our DES projects on Teacher Appraisal and School Development Plans, and our current school improvement project 'Improving the

Quality of Education for All'. I have also been fortunate to have worked over a slightly longer period with the OECD's Centre for Educational Research and Innovation on a number of school improvement-related projects. This work has helped me to see the teacher's role in the wider context of the school as an organization and workplace. In particular, it has impressed on me the crucial importance of the culture of the school in sustaining teacher development.

It is this commitment to a practical philosophy of emancipation and empowerment as well as a particular set of individual circumstances that underpin the argument in this book. After this introduction, a few case studies of teacher-based research are given to provide a context for what follows. In Chapter 3, two arguments are considered for teacher-based research – the need for professionalism in teaching, and the inadequacy of the traditional research approach in helping teachers improve their classroom practice. In Chapter 4, action research, which has become the main vehicle for teacher research, is discussed and critiqued; from that discussion, six criteria for teacher-based research are suggested. Chapter 5 discusses the ways in which teacher research problems are formulated and initiated. Chapters 6 and 7 describe the principles and practice of classroom observation, and in Chapter 8 various other ways of gathering information on classroom behaviour are described. Chapter 9 outlines a method for analysing this data. These five chapters constitute the heart of the teacher research process. Chapter 10 discusses ways in which classroom research can be reported, published and linked to the curriculum, teaching and staff development. The discussion in Chapter 11 links classroom research activities to current school improvement strategies, such as school self-evaluation, development planning and teacher appraisal. In the final chapter, I stand back a little and attempt briefly to connect the discussion in previous chapters to the themes of teacher and school development.

A continuing emphasis throughout the book is the importance of establishing a professional ethic for teaching.

Implicit in this idea is the concept of teacher as researcher. The teacher-researcher image is a powerful one. It embodies a number of characteristics that reflect on the individual teacher's capacity to be in Stenhouse's phrase 'autonomous in professional judgement'. A major factor in this is the teacher's ability to think systematically and critically about what he or she is doing and to collaborate with other teachers. Central to this activity is the systematic reflection on one's classroom experience, to understand it and to create meaning out of that understanding. By becoming self-conscious, collaborative and critical about their teaching, teachers develop more power over their professional lives and are better able to create classrooms and schools that are responsive to the vision they and we have for our children's future.

FURTHER READING

The key source for any teacher-researcher is the work of Lawrence Stenhouse, in particular his *An Introduction to Curriculum Research and Development* (1975). Although he died before making his own comprehensive statement on classroom research by teachers, Jean Rudduck and I (Rudduck and Hopkins 1985) edited his published and unpublished writing to make such an argument in *Research as a Basis for Teaching*. Until the mid-1980s most of the work on teacher research was either philosophical discussion (Kemmis 1982, 1983), reports by researchers (Elliot and Adelman 1976) or teachers' own accounts of their research (Nixon 1981). Since that time, however, there has been a dramatic growth in the number of books on the topic. Pride of place must go to John Elliott's (1991) *Action Research for Educational Change*, which traces the development of the teacher research movement, describes its methodology and explores how it can be 'a form of creative resistance' to centralized policy-making. Two other more recent books that attempt in different ways to link the ethic of teacher research to school development and educational change are Helen Simons' (1987) *Getting to Know Schools in Democracy* and our own *The Empowered School* (Hargreaves and Hopkins 1991). Although much else of relevance to the theme of 'classroom research by teachers' has been published recently, I have referred to them in the 'Further Reading' section at the end of the most appropriate chapter.

CHAPTER 2

Classroom Research in Action

Often the phrase classroom research brings to mind images of white-coated (or grey-suited!) educational researchers undertaking research in a sample of schools or classrooms and using as subjects the teachers and students who live out their educational lives within them. Often this image is correct. This book, however, is about another kind of research in which teachers look critically at their own classrooms primarily for the purpose of improving their teaching and the quality of education in their schools. But even the phrase 'classroom research by teachers' can sound a little daunting. It might be useful therefore to begin with some examples of teachers who have engaged in systematic self-conscious enquiry with the purpose of understanding and improving their practice.

The following four cases were all written by the teachers involved in the classroom research. The first two were prepared by teachers with whom I worked in British Columbia. They contrast well with each other: the first is an exploratory case study undertaken by a beginning teacher; the second is more focused, and reflects the confidence of a teacher experienced in classroom research.

The second pair of examples were written by teachers involved in the University of Cambridge Institute of Education and Bedfordshire Education Service 'Developing Successful Learning' Project. Besides describing different methodologies, they also illustrate the benefits of using partnerships in classroom research.

The final example is different from the others in a number of ways; in particular, it illustrates the use of 'quantitative' as opposed to the more usual 'qualitative' methods in teacher-based classroom research.

In each of these cases, the teachers are engaging in classroom research for the express purpose of improving the quality of educational life in their classroom. This is no deficit model of improvement, however; the teachers involved are genuinely interested in understanding the dynamics of their own teaching style. They believe that you do not have to be ill to get better. The motivation for doing so may be varied – a research degree, natural curiosity, a stimulating article or talk – but the process and its implications are essentially the same. Taken together, these cases illustrate the range and benefits of doing research in your own classroom and provide examples of the reflective professional in practice.

The first example is a case study by Sandra Meister, when she was a first year teacher in Prince George, British Columbia.

The purpose of this research project is to become familiar with educational research within the classroom, to analyse and improve one aspect of my teaching style. But I have had some difficulty in pinpointing which aspect of my teaching I wished to focus on. As a harried first year teacher, I really had not given much time to actually thinking about the way I taught; rather, I tended to worry about keeping things peaceful until the three o'clock bell rang. I decided, however, to look at the types of questions I asked, the order in which I asked them, and to whom the questions were directed. This sequence appears to be the key to training a child to think independently. In order to become more aware of my own teaching style, I decided to obtain data from myself as teacher, from my class and from an outside observer who was previously unknown to myself and my students.

Social studies was an area I find particularly dull at this level. The entire primary curriculum centres around 'myself and my family in our community', 'components of our community' and, finally, 'the interaction of communities'. The lessons I had taught were rather scattered and poorly sequenced. As a final unit, I decided to divide the class into three groups and have one group research communities of the past, one look at Prince George as it is today and one group design a community for the future. Most of the knowledge came from group lessons and discussions where, through various questions and brainstorming techniques, I hoped to direct the student to some logical conclusions as to the necessary requirements for community life.

The lesson used as the basis for the research was on different modes of communication. I taught the lesson while the observer recorded the types of questions asked (i.e. fact, critical thinking, explanation, yes/no, etc.), which students responded and the teacher reaction to the response. The data were gathered by the observer using a checklist. The lesson was also audio-taped, which enabled both the teacher and the observer to review the data afterwards.

The results were really quite an eye opener. The majority of my questions required critical thinking or an opinion, whereas the remainder were questions for the purpose of gathering facts. Most of the questions required one- or two-word answers. The following is an analysis of my questioning techniques.

Types of questions asked: on the positive side, most of the questions required critical thinking, i.e. 'How would you feel . . .?', 'What would you do if . . .?' Many questions required students to express an opinion; I avoided Yes/No questions, which is something I was pleased to note. On the negative side, I seemed to avoid asking any questions which required any type of explanation. This is an important area which I have overlooked.

Sequence of questions asked: the order in which the questions were asked seemed logical and new information was built on previous answers. The weakest area here seemed to be in moving from one topic to the next. I'll need to work on having a few key questions as pivot points for my lesson.

To whom questions were directed: on the positive side, I would often ask one question, such as 'Who do you talk to on the phone?', and randomly choose many students for a one-word answer which keeps them all involved and interested. On the negative side, whenever I asked an open question, I seemed to respond to one of three students regardless of who may have had their hands up. These particular students are those with whom I try and avoid confrontations.

Teacher responses to answers: this is the area which I feel this project has identified as something for me to question. As I looked at the data, I realized that I rarely praised the students verbally. The majority of teacher responses were repeating what the child said and nodding to affirm their stance. The next frequent teacher response was no reaction. The observer noted that the students seemed satisfied with the way their opinions were accepted without much comment and didn't appear to act differently when verbal praise was given. I also appeared to accept an answer regardless of whether hands were up or not.

There are three areas where the observer and I saw possibilities for improvement. The first is to accept answers and request answers from all students rather than a select few. An obvious way to improve this is to limit the size of the group to whom the lesson is being taught. Perhaps using a phrase such as 'let's let someone else have a turn' would help. The changes need not be large and I'm glad this was brought to my attention – imagine some poor child spending a year in my class and never being asked a question!

The second area for change is in making a smooth transition from one topic to the next within a lesson. I feel this can be accomplished by noting beforehand a comparison phrase or question and recording differences or similarities between the two topics.

Finally, I must learn to allow the children an opportunity to give detailed explanations. This is an ideal opportunity for improving verbal lucidity and compositional skills.

After some reflection on the research project, I feel that it was a valuable exercise. Having another individual working on the project immediately reduced the feelings of isolation I had from the staff. The other area that was most valuable was the opportunity to go through a research project under guidance from an experienced researcher. Now that contacts have been established, the feasibility of classroom research in Prince George has expanded. Having completed the process once makes a world of difference for considering future research projects.

The next time I conduct or participate in a research project, I will use the 'triangulation approach'. The insight of an outside observer is invaluable and also allows the students to offer some feedback. I would also like to participate in a project where the observer would be the director (adviser) and have more than one classroom involved. By playing a small role in a larger-scale project, I feel I would gain more first-hand knowledge and become confident in being a teacher-researcher.

The second case study is by Ann Waldo, an experienced teacher who had previously been involved in classroom research.

Bruce Joyce and Beverly Showers (1984) maintain that when given adequate training conditions, teachers are consistently able to fine-tune existing skills and learn new ones. However, they point out that learning a new skill does not guarantee being able to transfer a skill vertically to higher-order, more complex tasks. Early-task learning has been found to maxi-mize transfer if the tasks are relevant to the acquisition of a teaching model.

My school district has been encouraging teachers to use cognitive models of teaching. Bloom's Taxonomy and the Renzuli Triad Model have specifically been suggested as the models to be used to provide an enriched curriculum. Last year, teachers had in-service training on these approaches and this included theory and demonstration with adults. The demonstration teams were young, enthusiastic and well-prepared fellow teachers. The teachers went back to their classrooms ready to implement higher-order thinking. Despite using devices such as specific question words to elicit different levels of responses, most teachers found it very difficult to do this.

After watching a videotape of myself teaching and failing to allow students think-time before responding, I wondered if this inability in an early task could have caused some of the difficulties I experienced in using Bloom's Taxonomy and Renzuli's Triad Model, as both models are dependent on students' ability to articulate their thoughts. Verbalizing high-level thinking demands that time is spent formulating the response. The other two primary teachers in my school had only moderate success in implementing the new models.

I decided that for this piece of research I would ask these teachers consciously to extend think-time to the recom-mended 3–5 seconds. I hypothesized that this would lead to lengthier student responses and higher-order questions from the teacher. Hopefully, the teachers would also begin to internalize this early-task learning and be better equipped to implement other models of teaching that are dependent on student response.

The subjects were a grade 1 teacher (S1) who has taught for 27 years and a grade 2 teacher (S2) who has taught for 14 years. Both agreed to audiotape a session of directed reading to provide baseline data. They were informed that they would be asked to alter one aspect of their teaching which, in turn, was expected to cause a change to occur. It was decided that allowing the teachers to audiotape themselves would disturb students and teachers less than an observer or a videotape. S2 taped a group with low academic ability; S1 taped a group with average ability.

The baseline tapes were interpreted by myself. Think-time between each teacher question and response was recorded. If a response came less than 1 second after the question, it was designated 0 seconds. The number of words in each student response was counted. Each question was related to level 1, 2, 3, 4, 5 or 6 responses according to Bloom's Taxonomy. The hierarchy in Blooms's Taxonomy is: 1, knowledge; 2, comprehension; 3, application; 4, analysis; 5, synthesis; 6, evaluation. As S1 had taped only 13 questions and responses, I decided to use the first 10 questions on each tape, provided they were not repetitions or rephrasings.

These data were discussed with the teachers on the following day except for the hierarchical rating of the questions. This was not mentioned. They were asked to read an excerpt from 'Extending think-time for better reading instruction' by Linda Gambrell (1981). In this excerpt, the author stresses that the teacher must be prepared for leaden silences and resist the temptation to fill them. The student must also be prepared by the teacher to accept the think-time for thinking instead of unproductive hand-waving in the belief that responding is a speed competition. Lastly, she stresses that it takes time for teachers and students to slow down. There was no mention of higher levels of questions or responses.

The teachers, therefore, were set to extend think-time in the hope of lengthening student responses. They were asked to tape themselves three more times with the same reading groups, but it was explained that these tapes would be used for self-monitoring rather than as data. They were encouraged to extend think-time whenever appropriate in the classroom in order to get more practice.

Six school days after the baseline data had been collected, the teachers were again asked to tape their guided reading in order to provide data for the research. They were reminded to

Table 2.1

	Teacher	Think-time[a] (seconds)	Responses[a] (words)	Level[a]
Baseline	S1	0.1	2.4	1.2
	S2	1.0	3.5	1.4
Post-test	S1	2.5	4.6	1.5
	S2	3.2	6.3	1.5

[a] Average over ten questions.

use the same reading groups as for the baseline data. The data from these tapes were used in exactly the same manner as the baseline tapes.

For both teachers, there was an increase in the length of student response when think-time was increased (see Table 2.1). There was also a small increase in the hierarchical level of questions posed to the students by the teachers. These results cannot be said to be statistically significant because of the size of sample, but they do replicate other findings. The results would seem to indicate that teachers automatically ask more stimulating questions when they are consciously trying to increase student input into discussions.

One of the problems in the research design was that it did not allow for differences in conceptual ability. A teacher automatically adjusts level of questions according to the ability of the group. S2 could not change her level of questions too much because of the conceptual level of the group. S1 had an average group and could, therefore, hope to have higher-level responses even though the children were younger.

If I had had more time, I would have analysed far more data for each teacher and increased the number of teachers and done another piece of research to discover if there was any transfer effect using an information-processing model of teaching.

The third case describes how three teachers used a process of mutual support and observation to change teaching and learning experiences in their classrooms. Two of them, Sheelagh Sullivan and Liz Satherly, were teachers working in Samuel Whitbread Upper School. The third member of the group, Jackie Markham, had worked with teachers in the school as part of her role with the Special Education Support Service.

The partnership between Liz and Sheelagh developed because Sheelagh, as a learning support teacher, had worked in the classroom with Liz, a teacher of Humanities. Liz was a relatively new entrant to the profession and keen to develop more successful learning in her classroom. Sheelagh and Jackie were both keen to look at support for learning as a way of meeting individual needs.

Sheelagh and Liz had an informal meeting to discuss those aspects of their practice that they hoped to explore. Liz wanted to look at her classroom management and Sheelagh was concerned with effective group work. We also organized suitable times, lessons and classes for observation. It was difficult to fit in all of the desired observations, so Jackie offered to assist by taking on three of the observations. We spent some time discussing suitable observation techniques and decided that, to look at group work, we needed to use a video.

We wanted the opportunity to include some feedback from the students and so a last minute decision was made to use a brief questionnaire. A published questionnaire was used, but on reflection it would have better to have constructed our own.

The observations took place over a period of two weeks. Four of Liz's lessons were observed, two by Sheelagh and two by Jackie. Three of Sheelagh's were observed, one by Jackie and two by Liz using a video for the final observation. The video proved useful but there were some problems. We had not anticipated problems with lighting, sound discrimination, the intrusive nature of video and the recorder's sheer weight. The observations went well, the only difficulty being the lack of time for immediate feedback at the end of the lesson. The subsequent review meeting took longer than we had expected. It should have been obvious that a video of a one-hour lesson would take the same amount of time to watch!

In both cases, a descriptive feedback of the lesson was given. We avoided judgemental comments, although this sometimes felt impersonal. Both classroom teachers felt the need to hear about successful aspects of the lesson. They were able to identify specific areas of their practice where change could lead to more successful student learning.

Three roles developed during the course of these meetings: teacher, observer and 'critical friend'. These roles were interchangeable, but the critical friend tended to be the person who was able to ask leading questions that enabled the teacher to clarify her thinking and make decisions about the action she would take. Liz decided that she would give written instructions at the start of the lesson but would also provide supportive oral reinforcement at planned intervals. Sheelagh decided to remove barriers to communication by reorganizing seating arrangements and reducing group size. At this stage, it would have been useful to look at the questionnaires, but there had not been enough time to tabulate the results.

Liz and Sheelagh agreed to one further observation of each other's lessons, which would be followed by a meeting to reflect upon what had been achieved. Sheelagh managed to observe the lesson as planned, but practical obstacles made it impossible for Liz to reciprocate. However, we met as planned. It proved a very positive meeting. Sheelagh gave feedback to Liz and provided a self-evaluation of her own lesson. Many of the comments made at this stage were judgemental, but because of the level of trust and confidence that had been established, we didn't find this threatening. Also, because the discussion was so open, Jackie's role as critical friend disappeared.

Generally, we felt pleased with what had been achieved. Liz was convinced that the quality of coursework assignments produced by the group observed had improved. Further observations would be difficult to arrange, but it was felt that partnerships had been established through which an open discussion of teaching and learning experiences in our classrooms would be possible.

The fourth case was prepared by Pamela Hughes, a teacher of English and Sharnbrook Upper School's Individual Needs Co-ordinator.

During our initial 'chats', we decided that we would like to involve our students as much as possible; we were all learners. We were nervous about how the students would react to this approach, especially one class which contained some very 'strong characters', but we felt that it was important for us to involve them.

During the lesson prior to the observation, the students were asked to make lists of all the things that (a) helped and (b) hindered their understanding and learning in school, not just the class they were in for that lesson. There was a short class brainstorm before dividing into groups of four. The students, without exception, were animated and very enthusiastic and did not use this as an opportunity to be vindictive. The results gave us a useful insight into the students' perceptions of their learning as well as forming a 'learning bond' between us.

The observation

My lesson to be observed was a year 9 English class of 30 students, who would be working in groups carrying out tasks associated with beginnings of stories. I arrived to find no class, a sixth-former who had come to support without my prior knowledge, the furniture completely rearranged, a lack of chairs and my partner ready to observe my lesson! Once these minor setbacks had been overcome, I was ready to begin. I felt very conscious of another person in the very small claustrophobic room and I found myself being very careful about what I said and how I said it, but within a few minutes I had forgotten that I was being observed.

Christine wrote down a 'description' of my lesson, using words and diagrams, a mirror image, that we would use together for the Review. Immediately after the lesson, Christine thanked me for letting her observe my lesson and I felt relaxed and reassured. We confirmed our time for the Review.

The review

We decided to meet after school in Christine's classroom where we knew that we would not be disturbed. We reflected on my lesson and I did not feel threatened by the discussion. I began by giving my view of the lesson and then gradually we drew out areas that I could develop. I had challenged the able pupils by questioning, but the weaker students may have benefited from key ideas and words being put on the board to enable them to contribute more easily to their group discussions. Christine had noticed that one pair seemed 'inadequate' until the second task when they joined with another pair, and even then the four were not as creative or perceptive as the other groups. She also noticed an individual student on the fringes of his group discussion.

The action phase

I decided to review and develop two aspects of my teaching: my use of the board as a learning resource (not only within group work) and the management of groups within the class. My aim was to enable all students to participate fully when doing cooperative group tasks. To help evaluate whether these areas of development would be effective, we decided that I would give a questionnaire to the students as soon as possible and again during the second half of the term. I would monitor the progress of the three students mentioned by Christine. Also, a further observation would take place.

The reflection

Since our initial observations, Christine and I often discuss aspects of our lessons, not only those of our Action Plan, sharing success as well as conferring when needing support. We are at the stage of evaluating our initial Action Plans and feel confident that we will continue our partnership as we feel that we have learnt from each other and the students.

Christine's thoughts

I had worked in an Australian system where peer assessment was used in conjunction with appraisal by the senior management, in order to be re-licensed or promoted. This also involved a great deal of paperwork at first; therefore, I was apprehensive about forming a partnership with Pamela.

In fact, it has been like an 'ego-massage'! As teachers, we seldom have the opportunity of hearing another teacher's view of our classroom, or of observing another class ourselves. It has been a wonderful opportunity to recall success and discuss 'failures'. It has made us find time to listen and support each other; unless you make time there isn't any.

Our department is very open and people other than teachers and class members are often in the classroom, but this was different – it was for us. We were able to look at our teaching and the students in a different light. I was aware of a temptation to 'play to the new adult audience', but this disappeared quickly. The most singular thing to me is how memorable that lesson was; I feel that heightening my awareness at the time has helped memory of it to remain vivid.

When I went into Pamela's lesson I was a little apprehensive. I knew that I could walk into any of her lessons, but this was different as I felt that I was watching for something – looking for some area to define and not being certain what it was. This proved to be an unfounded concern. I mirrored the lesson as I saw it and we had plenty to review and debate.

We learnt from each other, opening up many possibilities. The lessons I observed and those I was observed in, are imprinted on my mind.

The final example is taken from a paper by Lawrence Stenhouse (1979: 71–77) (reprinted by permission of Universitetsforlaget AS). He describes, in the first person singular, the fictionalized predicament of a teacher who turns to the research literature for advice on which teaching strategy to use.

I teach social studies in the form of a human issues programme covering such topics as the family, poverty, people and work, law and order, war and society, relations between the sexes. I wonder whether I should include race relations. A complicating factor is my style of teaching controversial issues to adolescent students. I set up discussions and use evidence such as newspapers, stories, pamphlets, photographs and films. I act as neutral chairman in those discussions, in order to encourage critical attitudes without taking sides. In short, I have been influenced by and am in the tradition of the English Humanities Curriculum Project (Stenhouse 1970).

I am very concerned that my teaching should contribute positively to race relations in my multiracial society, if that is possible. I wonder whether I should teach about race relations at all. If so, I wonder whether it is appropriate in this case to take the role of neutral chairman, even though this is a teaching convention and not a position professing personal neutrality. So I turn to a research report on 'Problems and Effects of Teaching about Race Relations' for enlightenment (Stenhouse *et al.* 1982).

Here I find that the project has monitored on a pre-test, post-test basis two different strategies of teaching about race relations, one in which the teacher is neutral (called strategy A), the other in which the teacher feels free to express, whenever he feels it appropriate, his committed stance against racism (called strategy B). Strategy A was conducted in fourteen schools and strategy B in sixteen schools. The samples are not true random samples because of problems of accessibility of schools and students, but I know something about this from my study of education at college (Campbell and Stanley 1963). Control groups have been gathered in the same schools as the experimental groups whenever this was possible, though this was not possible in all cases. I came across this table (see Table 2.2) of results on a scale purporting to measure general racism.

This seems to help me a good deal at first sight. My neutral strategy is strategy A. Attitudes in the strategy A group seem to improve and, though the improvement does not quite reach even the 0.05 level of significance, the control groups, left to general influences, deteriorate in attitude significantly and the comparison of experimental and control shows at least by one criterion a 0.01 level discrimination in favour of teaching about race relations by strategy A. Strategy B does not look markedly superior to strategy A, so I don't seem to need to change my teaching style. So it seems that research has helped me by enabling me to decide the right style in which to teach about race relations.

But, oh dear, here's a problem. On a later page the same data are presented in a different form to show the situation in individual schools and this seems to complicate the issue as shown in Table 2.3. Now, looking at this table, I personally feel that, given comment codes A, B or C, I certainly ought to proceed, given comment codes D and possibly E, I should proceed with great care, and given codes F and G, I might be better to give a lot more thought to the matter. In seven out of twelve schools, the result seems encouraging, in four schools results seem doubtful and in one of the twelve rather alarming. How do I know what category my school will fall

Table 2.2 Scores on the general Racism Scale of the Bagley-Verma Test[a]

Teaching style	Experimental sample			Control sample			t-value for difference between the experimental and control groups
	Pre-test mean (S.D.)	Post-test mean (S.D.)	Direction of shift and t-value for difference of means	Pre-test mean (S.D.)	Post-test mean (S.D.)	Direction of shift and t-value for difference of means	
Strategy A							
Experimental (n = 258)	17.24 (10.05)	16.51 (10.25)	1.71				2.83**
Control (n = 124)				16.06 (9.66)	17.61 (10.49)	2.11*	
Strategy B							
Experimental (n = 359)	17.25 (9.61)	16.17 (9.78)	2.27				1.91
Control (n = 180)				17.42 (9.93)	17.87 (10.58)	0.72	

[a] A decrease in score represents a decrease in racism.
* $P < 0.05$; ** $P < 0.01$.

Table 2.3 Differences between pre- and post-test school means for the experimental and control groups on the General Racism (GR), Anti-Asian (AA) and Anti-Black (AB) scales of the Bagley-Verma Test: Strategy A

1 School code	2 Experimental GR	3 Experimental AA	4 Experimental AB	5 Control GR	6 Control AA	7 Control AB	8 Comment code
03	−1.83	−0.35	−1.22	–	–	–	C
07**	1.58	0.54	0.31	−0.86	0.21	−0.71	G
09	−0.22	0.55	−0.90	2.11	1.45	1.09	A
10*	−0.63	−0.18	−1.54	–	–	–	C
13	−0.85	0.37	−1.29	−0.89	−0.56	−0.67	D
17	−2.50	−1.17	−1.78	–	–	–	C
18	1.70	2.40	0.90	6.63	4.38	3.75	B
19	0.37	−0.04	0.62	–	–	–	D
29	−3.42	−1.75	−1.67	–	–	–	A
31**	−0.12	0.77	0.65	2.0	0.87	−0.25	D
32**	−1.61	−0.70	−0.83	0.34	0.50	−1.16	A
39*	1.20	−0.50	1.05	−0.07	−0.77	−0.38	D
Mean of strategy A controls (individuals)				(1.30)	(0.83)	(0.49)	

* 5–25% non-white; ** over 25% non-white.

Table 2.4 Differences between pre- and post-test school means for the experimental and control groups on the General Racism (GR), Anti-Asian (AA) and Anti-Black (AB) scales of the Bagley-Verma Test: Strategy B

1 School code	2 Experimental GR	3 Experimental AA	4 Experimental AB	5 Control GR	6 Control AA	7 Control AB	8 Comment code
01	-3.51	-1.60	-2.57	-1.75	1.43	-1.34	A
02	0.00	-0.67	-0.10	2.43	1.22	1.43	A
04*	1.04	0.10	0.24	–	–	–	E
05	-2.27	-0.34	-0.97	–	–	–	C
06*	-2.00	1.29	-1.30	0.55	0.34	-0.52	D
08	1.09	0.30	0.07	-5.40	-1.20	-2.33	G
09	-2.89	-0.22	-1.97	2.11	1.45	1.09	A
11	-1.58	-0.48	-0.53	–	–	–	C
14**	-0.33	0.39	0.91	–	–	–	D
15	-2.25	0.17	-1.42	–	–	–	C
20	-0.39	0.05	-0.22	-1.15	0.86	-1.43	F
21	-1.77	-1.32	-1.19	1.59	1.04	0.59	A
24*	0.19	0.37	0.60	4.93	1.07	1.65	B
30*	3.79	1.27	2.16	–	–	–	E
33	1.00	0.43	0.38	-0.83	0.83	-0.08	G
Mean of strategy B controls (individuals)				0.90	0.71	0.30	

* 5–25% non-white; ** over 25% non-white.

into? This is really rather disturbing for my decision. Perhaps I should shift to strategy B. Let's look at the strategy B Table (see Table 2.4).

Oh dear! This is no better. Here eight out of fifteen schools are reassuring, three are doubtful and three are alarming. Strategy B seems no refuge.

Can it be that statistically significant discriminations between two treatments when presented through means and standard deviations can mask such a range of within-sample variance as this? It can indeed. In the psychostatistical research paradigm, the effects are not 'other things being equal'; they are 'by and large' or 'for the most part'. So doing one thing is only sometimes better than doing the other! This, apparently, depends on your school context or school environment or perhaps yourself or your pupils.

What I have to find out now is whether teaching about race relations by strategy A is good for my pupils in my school. However, that reminds me that I haven't looked at pupils as individuals, only as means and standard deviations. Suppose I took these data and looked at them in a way that depicted the fate of individuals. How about a histogram of change scores. There are, of course, problems with such scores but, bearing them in mind, I'll give it a go (see Figs 2.1 and 2.2).

My goodness, it looks as if the same teaching style and the same subject matter make some people worse as they make other people better. One man's meat is another man's poison. If I teach about race relations, some people get worse. But if I refuse to teach about race relations, even more people get worse. I suppose I should have thought of that anyway. I know that when I teach literature some people come not to like it, but I believe that even fewer would enjoy literature if I didn't introduce them to it all.

I need to steady myself. After all, engineers don't always build exactly the same bridge. Nor do chess players always play the same game. There must be ways of fitting action to situation and perhaps even to individuals in that situation.

I've clearly got to think things out for myself. Does this mean that research cannot help me? What was that piece in

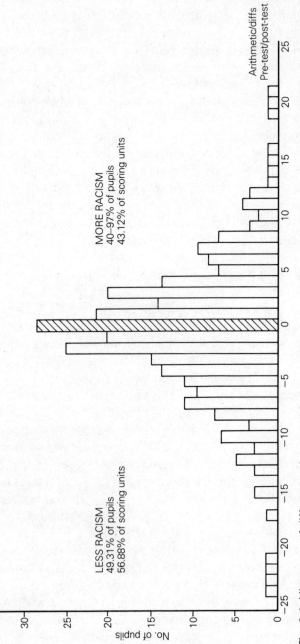

Fig. 2.1 Histogram of differences between the pre- and post-test scores on the General Racism scale of the Bagley-Verma test: Strategy A experimental ($n = 288$).

Fig. 2.2 Histogram of differences between the pre- and post-test scores on the General Racism scale of the Bagley-Verma test: Strategy A control (*n* = 128).

the paper by Cronbach they gave us in Ed. Psych? Here are my notes. And here it is:

> When we give proper weight to local conditions, any generalization is a working hypothesis, not a conclusion. (Cronbach 1975: 125)

That seems to mean that the results of research need testing in local conditions. What research gives me is most often not findings about all teaching but hypotheses about my teaching.

This is a bit of a shock, but it makes reasonable enough sense. And the hypotheses I've got are already of some use. I must test whether strategy A works well for me in my classroom, whether I can sustain its logic in practice and whether it is giving good results in attitudes. At the same time, I know that even in a good result some individuals may be deteriorating in attitude.

What I am going to do is this. I'm getting a student to come in and pre- and post-test my pupils and a control group in my school. But I'm also going to tape our sessions on race relations on a portable cassette-recorder. To do this, I have to tape other lessons too, so that I don't seem to be concentrating on race. I've started this. I'm explaining to the students that I'm doing a study of my own teaching and that this should help me to teach better. And I'm beginning to get them talking about how well my teaching and their learning goes.

Of course, there's a problem about how to handle the tapes. I played some at home and tried a Flanders Interaction Analysis (Flanders 1970) on them. It did tell me that I talked too much, but not a lot more. Then I tried the Humanities Curriculum Project analysis, which worked quite well because I was involved in discussion teaching. But I want to look at pupil behaviour as well as teacher behaviour. I'm beginning to ask myself whether I can develop a theory of individuals who cause me concern in class. I don't even need paper to do that. I can play cassettes in my car as I drive to and from work.

The more I come to study my own classroom, and my own school as well, the more I come to understand why the research provides case studies of classrooms. Comparing other people's experiences with my own throws up all sorts of illuminating possibilities – hypotheses, I mean.

At the end of this session, I'm going to try to set up a club in the district for teacher-researchers. They have clubs for people who tinker with motorcycles to get more performance from them, so why not the same for teachers who are tinkering with their teaching?

I'd like to set about testing Piaget. Most of his experiments are a kind of teaching. And I have a feeling that if I work with a small sample, like he did, I'll find out quite a lot for myself. I've got a better laboratory than he had: it's a real classroom!

I'm not sure if I'm doing research. I am testing hypothesis by experiment as systematically as a busy job allows.

The *Shorter Oxford English Dictionary* says that research is: 'Investigation, inquiry into things. Also, habitude of carrying out such investigation.' Well, it is beginning to become a habit.

FURTHER READING

There are a number of sources for further examples of classroom research by teachers. In *A Teacher's Guide to Action Research*, Jon Nixon (1981) presents a series of descriptive accounts by teachers of a variety of classroom research projects. Extended illustrations of teacher research are given by Michael Armstrong (1980) in *Closely Observed Children*. Classic examples of classroom research in this tradition, although involving the participation of an external researcher, are found in Smith and Geoffrey's (1968) *The Complexities of an Urban Classroom* and Stephen Rowland's (1984) *The Enquiring Classroom*. Jean Rudduck and her colleagues (Hull *et al.* 1985; May and Rudduck 1983; Rudduck 1981) have produced collections of teacher research accounts as a result of their funded research projects. The Classroom Action Research Network (CARN), the Ford Teaching Project, and the Teacher–Pupil Interaction and the Quality of Learning (TIQL) project (Ebbutt and Elliott 1985; Elliott and Ebbutt 1985a,b) all publish accounts of their classroom research activities which are available from the Centre for Applied Research in Education, University of East Anglia. More recent collections of teacher research case studies are found in *Action Research in Classrooms and Schools* (Hustler *et al.* 1986), which mainly focuses on secondary schools, and Rosemary Webb's (1990) *Practitioner Research in the Primary School*. Two other books that contain detailed examples of classroom research as well as descriptions of method and philosophical discussions are *Collaborative Action Research* (Oja and Smulyan 1989) and Richard Winters' (1989) *Learning from Experience*.

CHAPTER 3

Why Classroom Research by Teachers?

In asking the question, 'Why classroom research by teachers?', one is raising a whole series of issues around the topics of professionalism, classroom practice, the social control of teachers and the usefulness of educational research. Each of these issues provides a rationale for teacher research. For example, classroom research by teachers can be justified by references to professionalism because systematic self-study is a hallmark of those occupations that enjoy the label 'professional'. Unfortunately, the teacher's claim to professionalism sometimes falters at this definition. In this chapter, however, I will focus on two other themes that justify and, indeed, make imperative a concept of classroom research by teachers. The first is the link between classroom research by teachers and the establishing and refining of professional judgement. The second is the inappropriateness of the traditional research paradigm for helping teachers improve their teaching.

'AUTONOMOUS IN PROFESSIONAL JUDGEMENT'

Lawrence Stenhouse (1984: 69) described the ideal role of the teacher like this:

> Good teachers are necessarily autonomous in professional judgement. They do not need to be told what to do. They are not professionally the dependents of researchers or superintendents, of innovators or supervisors. This does not mean that they do not welcome access to ideas created by other people at other places or in other times. Nor do they reject advice, consultancy or support. But they do know that ideas and people are not of much real use until they are digested to the point where they are subject to the teacher's own judgement In short, it is the task of all educationalists outside the classroom to serve the teachers; for only teachers are in the position to create good teaching.

This is a very different image from the contemporary approach to schooling that is based on the assumption that instructions issued from the top – from the minister, the chief education officer or head – are put into practice at the appropriate level lower down the organization. This approach to education tends to equate schools to factories which operate on a rational input–output basis, with pupils as raw material, teachers as mechanics, the curriculum as the productive process and the school leaders as factory managers.

This image of schooling stands in direct contrast to the aspirations of the teacher research movement. John Elliott (in Nixon 1981: 1) has observed that 'the teacher as researcher movement emanated from the work and ideas of Lawrence Stenhouse'. Crucial to an understanding of Stenhouse's intellectual position is, as we saw in Chapter 1, the notion of emancipation (see Stenhouse 1983). In this context, emancipation refers to the process involved in liberating teachers from a system of education that denies individual dignity by returning to them some degree of self-worth through the exercise of professional judgement. In terms of curriculum and teaching, the path to emancipation involves reconceptualizing curriculum development as curriculum research, and the linking of research to the art of teaching (Rudduck and Hopkins 1985). When viewed through this particular lens, centrally imposed curricula are in danger of becoming prescriptive blueprints that tend to inhibit autonomy in teaching and learning. On the other hand, the process model of curriculum, as described by Stenhouse (1975), is liberating or emancipatory because it encourages independence of thought and argument on the part of the pupil, and experimentation and the use of judgement on the part of the teacher. When teachers adopt this experimental approach to their teaching, they are taking on an educational idea, cast in the form of a curriculum proposal, and testing it out within their classrooms. As Stenhouse (1975: 142) said:

> The crucial point is that the proposal is not to be regarded as an unqualified recommendation but rather as a provisional specification claiming no more than to be worth putting to the test of practice. Such proposals claim to be intelligent rather than correct.

The major consequence of doing this is that teachers take more control of their professional lives. Not content to be told what to do or being uncertain about what it is one is doing, teachers who engage in their own research are developing their professional judgement and are moving towards emancipation and autonomy. Although this approach encourages new teaching strategies and implies a different way of viewing knowledge, it is not inimical to the idea of a National Curriculum.

Successful implementation of any centralized innovation requires adaptation by teachers at the school level. It is not an either/or situation or a straight choice between 'top-down' or 'bottom-up' – it is a combination of both. As

Denis Lawton (1989: 85) argues in his book *Education, Culture and the National Curriculum*:

> [we need] more curriculum development which is at least partly school-based. This is not to suggest that the centre–periphery or 'top-down' models of curriculum development are completely outmoded: it is a question of balance. It would be unreasonable to expect every school to develop its own curriculum from first principles, but it would be equally foolish to attempt to impose a detailed, uniform curriculum on every school, leaving no room for school-based development geared to specific local needs.

This balance is maintained through the professionalism of teachers. As Lawton (1989: 89) further comments:

> The increasing desire of teachers to be treated as professionals rather than as state functionaries, has encouraged a tendency to look for ways in which teachers could solve their own professional problems at a local level rather than react to more remote initiatives. Hence the emphasis on the school as the obvious location for curriculum renewal, the in-service education of teachers, the evaluation of teaching and learning, and even educational research.

In recent years, with the increase in centralized innovation and change, many teachers have found themselves involved in schemes for school self-review, curriculum evaluation, development planning, teacher appraisal and so on. All of these activities, as is argued in Chapter 11, build on classroom research techniques. When viewed in this way, they can provide further powerful opportunities for contributing towards the development of a teacher's professional judgement and the quality of education in their schools.

PROBLEMS IN TRADITIONAL APPROACHES

Perhaps the most unfortunate aspect of traditional educational research is that it is extremely difficult to apply its findings to classroom practice. The final case study in Chapter 2 is a good illustration of this. In a quandary about which teaching strategy to use, the fictionalized teacher went to the research literature for guidance. His subsequent experience was as frustrating as it was predictable, because the literature contains few unequivocal signposts for action. This dilemma is widespread: teachers quite rightly (in most cases) regard educational research as something irrelevant to their lives and see little interaction between the world of the educational researcher and the world of the teacher.

Arthur Bolster (1983: 295) asks the question, 'Why has research on teaching had so little influence on practice?', and his response to the question is worth quoting:

> The major reason, in my opinion, is that most such research, especially that emanating from top-ranked schools of education, construes teaching from a theoretical perspective that is incompatible with the perspective teachers must employ in thinking about their work. In other words, researchers and school teachers adopt radically different sets of assumptions about how to conceptualize the teaching process. As a result, the conclusions of much formal research on teaching appear irrelevant to classroom teachers – not necessarily wrong, just not very sensible or useful. If researchers are to generate knowledge that is likely to affect classroom practice, they must construe their inquiries in ways that are much more compatible with teachers' perspectives.

Most researchers when they enter classrooms bring with them perspectives derived from academic disciplines. Their view of how knowledge evolves and how it is determined are firmly established by their formal training. The world view that guides researchers' actions is consequently at odds with that of teachers. The teacher derives his or her knowledge of teaching from continual participation in situational decision making and the classroom culture in which they and their pupils live out their daily lives. So one reason why traditional educational research is of little use to teachers is because of the differing conceptions of teaching held by teachers and researchers. But there are other problems.

Research in education is usually carried out within the psycho-statistical research paradigm. This implies tightly controlled experimentation and the testing of hypotheses by assessing the effectiveness of a treatment across randomly selected groups through the use of statistical analysis. This approach is based on the agricultural research designs of R. A. Fisher (1935) in the 1930s. At that time, educationalists, desiring to link research to action, began to utilize the very successful 'agricultural–botany' designs of Fisher in educational settings. This has continued (and increased) down to the present day as can be seen by the myriad of postgraduate theses that use this research design. The basic idea underlying Fisher's designs is that experiments are conducted on samples, usually divided into a control and an experimental group, with the results generalized to the target population. The point is that samples are randomly drawn and are consequently representative of that target population.

Stenhouse (1979) describes Fisher's approach like this:

> The strength of Fisher's paradigm is the recognition of random sampling, in which a sample is drawn such that each member of the target population has an equal chance of being included in the sample because it is a device of chance. . .
>
> In Fisher's agricultural setting, the hypotheses were not derived from scientific theory. . . They were hy-

potheses regarding the relative effectiveness of alternative procedures, and the criteria of effectiveness was gross crop yield.

The result of an experiment of this kind is an estimate of the probability that – other things being equal – a particular seed strain or fertilizer or amount of watering will result in a higher gross yield than an alternative against which it has been tested. . . It is in applying experimental methods to teaching and curriculum evaluation in the schools that researchers have used the Fisherian model. The assumption is that one teaching procedure or curriculum can be tested against alternatives as a seed strain or fertilizer can in agriculture, i.e. procedures can be tested against yield without a real theoretical framework.

This approach to educational research is problematic, particularly if its results are to be applied to classrooms. First, it is extraordinarily difficult to draw random samples in educational settings (e.g. a random sample of schools, pupils and teachers would have to be drawn separately). Second, there are a myriad of contextual variables operating on schools and classrooms (e.g. community culture, teacher personality, school ethos, socio-economic background, etc.) that would affect the results. Third, it is difficult to establish criteria for effective classroom or school performance. Even if one could resolve these difficulties, there are, as Stenhouse (1979) points out, two deeper problems that relate to the nature of educational activity.

First, the 'agricultural–botany' paradigm is based on measures of gross yield (i.e. how much produce can be gathered in total from a section of land). That is an inappropriate measure for education. As teachers, we are concerned with the individual progress of students rather than with aggregated scores from the class or the school. Our emphasis is on varying teaching methods to suit individual pupils in order to help them achieve to the limit of their potential. Stenhouse (1979: 79) puts the paradox like this:

> The teacher is like a gardener who treats different plants differently, and not like a large scale farmer who administers standardised treatments to as near as possible standardised plants.

The second deeper problem relates to meaningful action. The teacher–pupil or pupil–pupil interactions that result in effective learning are not so much the consequence of a standardized teaching method but the result of both teachers and pupils engaging in meaningful action. And meaningful action cannot be standardized by control or sample. This is a similar argument to the one commonly used against those who overrate the utility of behavioural objectives. Behavioural objectives provide an excellent means for the teaching of skills or evaluating rote learning, but they tend to be counter-productive with more complex and sophisticated content areas. In the instance of rote learning, one can accept the parallel with standardized treatments, but not so easily with poetry appreciation. Here pupil response is the result of individual negotiation with the subject, mediated through and by the teacher – namely, a form of meaningful action. In this case, education as induction into knowledge is, as Stenhouse (1975: 82) memorably points out, 'successful to the extent that it makes the behavioural outcomes of pupils unpredictable' and, therefore, not generalizable. The implications of this line of thinking for teacher-researchers is to encourage them to look outside the psycho-statistical paradigm for their research procedures.

To summarize, I have made two points in arguing that the traditional approach to educational research is not of much use to teachers. The first point is that teachers and researchers do not conceptualize teaching in the same way. They live in different intellectual worlds and so their meanings rarely connect. Secondly, the usual form of educational research, the psycho-statistical or agricultural–

botany paradigm, has severe limitations as a method of construing and making sense of classroom reality. For these two reasons, teachers and those concerned with understanding classroom life have increasingly adopted different approaches to classroom research.

Arthur Bolster (1983) advocates an ethnographic approach as the research methodology most likely to generate knowledge that is intellectually rigorous and helpful for teacher development. Stenhouse goes further than this and suggests not only a research approach that is grounded in the reality of classroom culture, but one that is under the control of teachers. I am calling this form of research in which teachers do research in their own classrooms for the purpose of improving practice, teacher research. The phrase, teacher research, has the advantage of being simple and identifies the major actor and the process involved. It is in this sense and with this aspiration that the terms 'classroom research by teachers', 'teacher-based research' and the 'teacher-researcher' are used in this book. It is the description of such an approach to classroom research that provides the substance of the following chapter.

FURTHER READING

The notion of professionalism used in this chapter comprises a major theme in two of Lawrence Stenhouse's books: *An Introduction to Curriculum Research and Development* (1975) and *Authority, Education and Emancipation* (1983). An important discussion of the historical background to the nature of teacher professionalism is included in Dan Lortie's (1975) *School Teacher*. An excellent wide-ranging discussion of the practical implications of professionalism is found in Donald Schon's (1983) *The Reflective Practitioner*. A more contemporary discussion of reflective professionalism in teaching is found in the contributions to *Quality in Teaching*, edited by Wilf Carr (1989). For a more detailed exposition of Stenhouse's critique of the traditional approach to educational research, see *Research as a Basis for Teaching* (Rudduck and Hopkins 1985). An entertaining and comprehensive review of the arguments against traditional educational research as well as an alternative approach is found in *Beyond the Numbers Game* (Hamilton *et al.* 1977). These arguments are also well rehearsed in Winters' (1989) *Learning from Experience*, Carr and Kemmis' (1986) *Becoming Critical* and Elliott's (1991) *Action Research for Educational Change*. A broader perspective on this 'alternative approach' to educational research is found in texts such as Lincoln and Guba's (1985) *Naturalistic Inquiry* and Sara Delamont's (1992) witty and perceptive *Fieldwork in Educational Settings*.

CHAPTER 4

Action Research and Classroom Research by Teachers

In the previous chapter, I outlined a series of problems associated with the traditional approach to educational research that limits its usefulness for teachers who wish to improve their practice. There are, however, at least two other research traditions to which teachers can turn. One tradition is associated with the work of sociologists and anthropologists. Social anthropological, ethnographic, phenomenological, naturalistic and illuminative research are examples of these research approaches. These are long words that describe essentially the same approach – one that attempts to understand a social situation and to derive hypotheses from that effort of appreciation. The procedures that such social scientists have developed for analysing fieldwork data are used in this book as a guide for making sense of classroom data. They are described in some detail in Chapter 9.

The other research tradition that stands in contrast to the psycho-statistical paradigm and has a strong link with contemporary social science research is the method known as action research. In recent years, teacher-researchers have adopted the label 'action research' to describe their particular approach to classroom research. In this chapter, I describe and critique this application of action research, and from the discussion propose six criteria for classroom research by teachers.

ACTION RESEARCH

Action research combines as substantive act with a research procedure; it is action disciplined by enquiry, a personal attempt at understanding while engaged in a process of improvement and reform.

Here are four definitions of action research. The first is by Robert Rapoport (1970), who says that action research:

> . . . aims to contribute both to the practical concerns of people in an immediate problematic situation and to the goals of social science by joint collaboration within a mutually acceptable ethical framework.

The second is by Stephen Kemmis (1983), who writes:

> Action research is a form of self-reflective enquiry undertaken by participants in social (including educational) situations in order to improve the rationality and justice of (a) their own social or educational practices, (b) their understanding of these practices, and (c) the situations in which the practices are carried out. It is most rationally empowering when undertaken by participants collaboratively, though it is often undertaken by individuals, and sometimes in cooperation with 'outsiders'. In education, action research has been employed in school-based curriculum development, professional development, school improvement programs, and systems planning and policy development.

The third is taken from a paper by Dave Ebbutt (1985), who not only gives a definition of his own, but also quotes from Kemmis. He writes that action research:

> ... is about the systematic study of attempts to improve educational practice by groups of participants by means of their own practical actions and by means of their own reflection upon the effects of those actions.

> Put simply action research is the way groups of people can organise the conditions under which they can learn from their own experience. (Kemmis)

> Action research is trying out an idea in practice with a view to improving or changing something, trying to have a real effect on the situation. (Kemmis)

The fourth is from John Elliott (1991: 69):

> Action-research might be defined as 'the study of a social situation with a view to improving the quality of action within it'. It aims to feed practical judgement in concrete situations, and the validity of the 'theories' or hypotheses it generates depends not so much on 'scientific' tests of truth, as on their usefulness in helping people to act more intelligently and skilfully. In action-research 'theories' are not validated independently and then applied to practice. They are validated through practice.

The development of the idea of action research is generally attributed to Kurt Lewin, who in the immediate post-war period used it as a methodology for intervening in and researching the major social problems of the day. Lewin maintained that through action research advances in theory and needed social changes might simultaneously be achieved. Action research, according to Lewin, 'consisted in analysis, fact-finding, conceptualisation, planning execution, more fact-finding or evaluation; and then a repetition of this whole circle of activities; indeed a spiral of such circles' (quoted in Kemmis 1982: 13).

Lewin's ideas on action research were almost immediately applied to education, as well as social science more generally. It was the work of Stephen Corey at Teacher's College, Columbia University, however – in particular, his book *Action Research to Improve School Practice* (1953) – that spread the word about action research into 'mainstream' American education.

More recently, action research has been seen as a methodology through which the aspirations of critical theory, which itself is regarded as an increasingly important trend in the philosophy of social science and the study of education, might be realized. Critical theory builds on the work of Marx, Freud and the traditions of the 'Frankfurt School' of philosophy, in particular the writings of Jurgen Habermas. Unfortunately, the outstanding characteristic of critical theory is its unintelligibility! This is a great pity as well as a paradox, because the central purpose of critical theory is emancipation – enabling people to take control and direction over their own lives. There are now, however, a number of books that admirably 'translate' critical theory and explore its educational implications. In one of them, Rex Gibson (1986: 5–6) describes the central characteristic of critical theory like this:

> Critical theory acknowledges the sense of frustration and powerlessness that many feel as they see their personal destinies out of their control, and in the hands of (often unknown) others. . . Critical theory attempts to reveal those factors which prevent groups and individuals taking control of, or even influencing, those decisions which crucially affect their lives. . . In the exploration of the nature and limits of power, authority and freedom, critical theory claims to afford insight into how greater degrees of autonomy could be available.

> This characteristic marks out critical theory's true distinctiveness: its claim to be *emancipatory*. Not only does it provide enlightenment (deeper awareness

of your true interests); more than that (indeed, because of that), it can set you free. Unlike scientific theory, it claims to provide guidance as to what to do.

If this all sounds too good to be true, Gibson goes on to warn us that:

> There are clearly immense problems attaching to a theory which not only argues that it reveals the world more clearly, but also asserts that it can be used to change the world, to liberate from inequalities and unfair restrictions.

Obviously, neither critical theory nor action research are panaceas and they should not be regarded as such. We shall continue to see in this book, however, that their practical applications do provide a rationale and method for teachers who wish to take more control of their professional (and personal) lives.

From even this brief description, it can be seen how the method of action research with its twin emphasis on committed action and reflection is particularly suited to putting into practice such an emancipatory philosophy. There is also a pleasing symmetry between this more abstract discussion and the practical educational philosophy of Lawrence Stenhouse, and those who have followed his lead, as we see in the following section.

MODELS OF ACTION RESEARCH

The combination of the action and the research components has a powerful appeal for teachers. In the UK, Lawrence Stenhouse was quick to point to the connection between action research and his concept of the teacher as researcher. Later, John Elliott popularized action research as a method for teachers doing research in their own classrooms through the Ford Teaching Project, and established the Classroom Action Research Network.

Recently, Stephen Kemmis has considerably refined and formalized the concept of action research and how it applies to education. Based at Deakin University in Australia, Kemmis and his colleagues have produced a series of publications and courses and materials on action research, curriculum development and evaluation. His articles on action research (Kemmis 1982, 1983) are a useful review of how educational action research has developed from the work of Lewin and established its own character. Of more interest to us here is his 'Action Research Planner' (Kemmis and McTaggart 1988), where a sequential programme for teachers intending to engage in action research is outlined in some detail. He summarizes his approach to action research in the model shown in Fig. 4.1.

My enquiry questioning is disrupted by my need to keep control in ways the class expects.

Record questions and responses on tape for a couple of lessons to see what is happening. Keep notes of my impressions in a diary.

Enquiry developing but students are more unruly. How can I keep them on track? By listening to each other, probing their questions? What lessons help?

Record on tape questioning and control statements. Note in diary effects on student behaviour.

My students think that science means recalling facts rather than a process of enquiry. How can I stimulate enquiry in my students? Change the curriculum? Change my questioning? Settle on questioning strategies.

Shift questioning strategy to encourage students to explore answers to their own questions.

Try questions which let students say what they mean, what interests them.

Continue general aim but reduce number of control statements.

Use less control statements for a couple of lessons.

PLAN

REFLECT

OBSERVE

ACT

REVISED PLAN

REFLECT

OBSERVE

ACT

Fig. 4.1 The 'action research spiral' (based on Kemmis and McTaggart 1988: 14).

John Elliott was quick to take up Kemmis' schema of the action research spiral and he, too, produced a similar but more elaborate model, as seen in Fig. 4.2. Elliott (1991: 70)

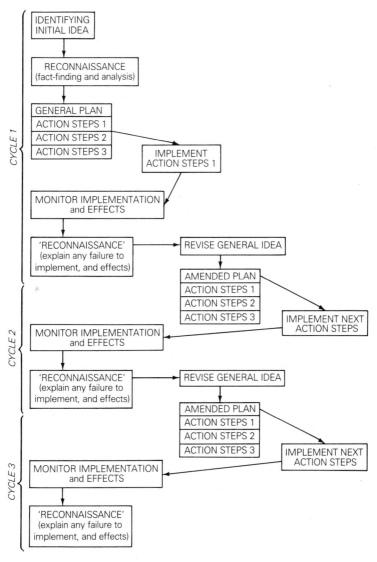

Fig. 4.2 Elliott's action research model (from Elliott 1991: 71).

summarizes Kemmis' approach and then outlines his elaborations like this:

> Although I think Kemmis' model is an excellent basis for starting to think about what action research involves, it can allow those who use it to assume that 'The General Idea' can be fixed in advance, that 'Reconnaissance' is merely fact-finding and that 'Implementation' is a fairly straightforward process. But I would argue that:
>
> 'The General Idea' should be allowed to shift.
>
> 'Reconnaissance' should involve analysis as well as fact-finding, and should constantly recur in the spiral of activities, rather than occur only at the beginning.
>
> 'Implementation' of an action-step is not always easy, and one should not proceed to evaluate the effects of an action until one has monitored the extent to which it has been implemented.

Dave Ebbutt (1985), a colleague of Elliott, provides us with another variation on Kemmis' model and makes these comments about it:

> It seems clear to me that Elliott is wrong in one respect, in suggesting that Kemmis equates reconnaissance with fact finding only. The Kemmis diagram clearly shows reconnaissance to comprise discussing, negotiating, exploring opportunities, assessing possibilities and examining constraints – in short there are elements of analysis in the Kemmis notion of reconnaissance. Nevertheless I suggest that the thrust of Elliott's three statements is an attempt on the part of a person experienced in directing action research projects to recapture some of the 'messiness' of the action-research cycle which the Kemmis version tends to gloss.

But Ebbutt (1985) claims that the spiral is not the most useful metaphor. Instead, the most:

. . . appropriate way to conceive of the process of action research is to think of it as comprising of a series of successive cycles, each incorporating the possibility for the feedback of information within and between cycles. Such a description is not nearly so neat as conceiving of the process as a spiral, neither does it lend itself quite so tidily to a diagrammatic represen- tation. In my view the idealized process of educational action research can be more appropriately represented like this: [as shown in Fig. 4.3]

A number of other similar models have recently been developed, most of which build on Lewin's original idea or Kemmis' interpretation of it. For example, James McKernan (1991) has suggested a 'time process' model (see Fig. 4.4) which emphasizes the importance of not allowing an action research 'problem' to become too rigidly fixed in time, and of rational problem solving and democratic ownership by the community of researchers.

My purpose in presenting these four practical models of action research is two-fold. Firstly, I intend to provide an overview of action research to help the reader gain an understanding of the whole process. Secondly, it is to demonstrate that despite the proliferation of eponymous 'models', they do, in fact, share more similarities than differences. There is a high degree of consensus among those who write on the subject about overall method and purpose. There are, however, some problems inherent in these models and to these I now turn.

CRITIQUE OF EDUCATIONAL ACTION RESEARCH

There are three main areas of concern that I have with the action research models developed by Kemmis, Elliott, Ebbutt, McKernan and others. Although this is not the place for a thoroughgoing critique, a brief discussion of

Idealized representation of the process of action research

Fig. 4.3 Ebbutt's model.

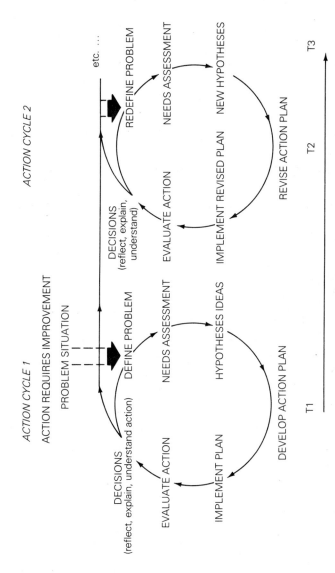

Fig. 4.4 McKernan's action research model (from McKernan 1991: 29).

these concerns is necessary because the problems may lead teacher-researchers into possible confusion. Also, the critique will help explain the form and structure of the rest of the book.

My first concern is that there may be a misunderstanding of the nature of Lewinian action research. As I mentioned earlier, the term action research was coined as a useful label to describe what teacher-researchers were doing. Recently, much energy has been devoted to setting out the intellectual basis for action research as it derived from Lewin. Lewin's conception of action research is, however, very different in some respects to what goes on in the name of teacher research. Lewin's concept of action research was (1) as an externally initiated intervention designed to assist a client system, (2) functionalist in orientation and (3) prescriptive in practice. None of these features apply to what I assume to be the nature of classroom research by teachers which is characterized by its practitioner, problem solving, and eclectic orientation.

I am also concerned about the values implicit in the Lewinian approach. The functionalist values that appear in his writing are in contrast to his commitment to democratic and communitarian values. It is doubly ironic that Kemmis illustrates the process of action research by citing Lewin's example of the bombing of German factories! Although Kemmis says that educational action research has moved away from Lewin's original ideas, I am still concerned that this emphasis will associate teacher research with a set of values that are at odds with its central emphasis on individual autonomy, action and 'emancipation'. We should take care that what began as a useful label to describe teacher research for professional development purposes does not assume a different character as a result of a quest for intellectual credibility.

My second concern relates to the specification of process in the action research models. There are three interrelated points. The first is that the tight specification of process steps and cycles may trap teachers within a framework which they may come to depend on and which will, consequently, inhibit independent action. The original purpose of teacher research was to free teachers from the constraints of prespecified research designs. It is useful to have a guide for action; my concern is when it becomes, or appears to become, prescriptive. Second, the models outline a process rather than a technology. They delineate a sequence of stages, but say little about the 'what' and the 'how' within these stages. Third, the models may appear daunting and confusing to practitioners. Ebbutt himself admits that Elliott's framework tends to mystification.

Unfortunately, models and frameworks cannot mirror reality: they are one individual's interpretation of reality. Consequently, they impose upon the user a prespecified analysis of a process that the user may quite rightly interpret differently. At best, they provide a starting point, an initial guide to action. At worst, they trap the practitioners within a set of assumptions that bear little relationship to their reality and, consequently, constrain their freedom of action.

The line between specifying principles of procedure that encourage informed action, and prescribing activities that determine behaviour and limit outcomes, is a very fine one indeed. There is a real danger that teacher research will assume the character of the objectives model, which '. . . is like a site-plan simplified so that people know exactly where to dig their trenches without having to know why' (Stenhouse 1980). To use Jean Rudduck's felicitous phrase, it seems that already 'the elusive butterfly of teacher research has been caught and pinned'.

My third concern is a semantic one. There is a tendency for some 'action researchers' to overuse words and phrases like *'problem'*, *'improve'*, *'needs assessment'* and so on. This could give the impression that action research is a deficit model of professional development. 'Something is wrong, so do this to make it better.' I know that this is not the intention, and I am as guilty of this as anyone in this regard, but it does behove all of us to talk (and write) about classroom research in as positive a way as we can. At the present time, the teaching profession in the UK is suffering from low morale largely as a result of ill-informed public and political criticism. Action research is one way of restoring and enhancing professional confidence.

These concerns notwithstanding, the importance of action research is not to be underestimated. Action research provides teachers with a more appropriate alternative to traditional research designs and one that is, in aspiration at least, emancipatory. We must, however, be aware of the problems associated with too prescriptive a framework for action and the values that are embedded within it. Consequently, I tend to use terms like 'classroom research by teachers' rather than action research. This is not a fundamental point of difference with those colleagues I have cited earlier. It does, however, serve to emphasize the importance of the acquisition of skills and techniques that become part of a teacher's repertoire and which are then subject to the exercise of his or her professional judgement.

CLASSROOM RESEARCH BY TEACHERS

My preference for the phrase 'classroom research by teachers' rather than 'action research' will not lead me to produce an alternative step-by-step model. Instead, I will present a series of methods and techniques that teachers can use in their classroom research efforts. In particular, I will discuss:

1 Ways in which classroom research projects can be identified and initiated (Chapter 5).
2 Principles and methods of classroom observation and of other ways of gathering data on classroom behaviours (Chapters 6–8).
3 Ways of interpreting and analysing the data gathered from classroom research (Chapter 9).
4 Ways in which the research process can be sustained (Chapter 10).

5 Ways in which classroom research methods can support and link to other school improvement initiatives (Chapter 11).

My purpose in tackling classroom research in this way is to give teachers an introduction to the variety of methods available to them as a means of extending their repertoire of professional practices and of encouraging flexibility in professional development. These are methods and approaches that teachers can put into use, that will empower them, and make them increasingly competent and 'autonomous in professional judgement'.

CRITERIA FOR CLASSROOM RESEARCH BY TEACHERS

The essence of what I am advocating is the development of a teacher's professional expertise and judgement. Although many teachers are in broad agreement with this general aim, some are quite rightly concerned about how far involvement in classroom research activity will impinge upon their teaching and on their personal time. Concerns are also raised as to the utilitarian or practical value of classroom research. With these concerns in mind, let me suggest the following six principles for classroom research by teachers.

The first is that the teacher's primary job is to teach, and any research method should not interfere with or disrupt the teaching commitment. This rule of thumb should serve to quell immediate concerns, but it also points to certain ethical considerations. In some instances, it may be inevitable that the adoption of a new and barely internalized teaching strategy is initially less effective than the way one previously taught. Is it ethical, therefore, some may ask, for a teacher to subject students to an inferior performance when the original behaviour was perfectly adequate? These are questions which ultimately can only be answered by the individuals involved. For my part, I am prepared to stand behind the teacher's judgement, particularly if the teachers involved are so concerned about improving the teaching and the learning experience of their students that they have broken the mould and are experimenting with new models. In becoming a teacher-researcher, the individual teacher is deliberately and consciously expanding his or her role to include a professional element. It is almost inconceivable, then, that he or she would do this and at the same time ignore the primacy of the teaching/learning process.

The second criterion is that the method of data collection must not be too demanding on the teacher's time. As a corollary, the teacher needs to be certain about the data collection technique before using it. The reasons for this are obvious. Teachers already consider themselves overworked and there are continuing demands for increased preparation and professional development time. It is naive to assume that the adoption of a research role will make no inroads on a teacher's private time. This can be reduced, however, by judicious use of specific data collection techniques, and the utilization of easily analysed diagnostic methods. For example, the tape-recorder is widely regarded as a very useful tool for the classroom researcher. It is, however, extremely expensive to use both in terms of time and money. It takes approximately 50 per cent longer to listen to a tape than to make it, and on top of that transcription (which is necessary if full use is to be made of the method) is both time-consuming and expensive. Given this, it is advisable to use another method for broad spectrum diagnosis and reserve such intensive techniques for specific and finely focused enquiries. A taxonomy of data collection techniques is presented in Chapter 6 and a number of techniques for classroom observation are discussed in Chapter 7.

The third criterion is perhaps the most contentious. The methodology employed must be reliable enough to allow teachers to formulate hypotheses confidently and develop strategies applicable to their classroom situation. Traditional researchers hold a poor opinion of action research. In many cases, that opinion is well-founded, particularly if it is based on individual pieces of research. It behoves all researchers, be they psycho-statisticians engaged in large-scale research or a primary teacher testing Piaget's theoretical hypotheses, to be rigorous about their methodology. It is no excuse at all to claim that rigour is unnecessary because the research is practitioner-oriented, small-scale or used solely to improve individual practice. If a change in teaching strategy is to be made, then that decision needs to be based on reliable data. These issues form the substance of Chapter 8.

The fourth criterion is that the research problem undertaken by the teacher should be one to which he or she is committed. Although this sounds self-evident, it is difficult enough, given all the pressures on a teacher's time, to sustain energy in a project even if it is intrinsically interesting and important to the teacher's professional activities. As a corollary, the problem must in fact be a problem; that is, the problem must be capable of solution, else by definition it is not a problem. If a teacher chooses a topic that is too complex or amorphous, then frustration and disillusionment will soon set in.

The fifth criterion refers to the need for teacher-researchers to pay close attention to the ethical procedures surrounding their work. Ethical standards for classroom researchers have been worked out over the past decade by researchers associated with the Centre for Applied Research in Education (e.g. MacDonald and Walker 1974; Simons 1982, 1987). A summary of ethical procedures for teacher-researchers can be found in the Appendix.

The sixth criterion is that as far as possible classroom research should adopt a 'classroom exceeding' perspective. What I mean by this is that all members of a school community actively build and share a common vision of their main purpose. Teachers collaborating on classroom research projects are now increasingly relating the focus of their classroom research efforts to whole school priorities through the use of classroom observation techniques. They adapt educational ideas and policies to suit their own context and professional needs. The main focus for action is the teaching and learning in classrooms, in order that *all* students develop 'the intellectual and imaginative powers and competencies' that they need in as personalized a way as possible. Such classroom practice can only be sustained through on-going staff development. These principles characterize an approach to teacher and school development that builds on the methods and philosophy of classroom research. In Chapters 10 and 11, we see how this can fit into an overall strategy for school improvement.

In the chapters that follow, these criteria will be dealt with in more detail. In the next chapter, the ways of developing a focus for classroom research projects are discussed.

FURTHER READING

One of the earliest examples of teacher-based research was the Humanities Curriculum Project and the approach is still worth considering (Stenhouse 1970, 1983). Of similar interest are the accounts of the Ford Teaching Project (Elliott and Adelman 1976) and the materials from Deakin University, for example their *Action Research Reader* (1982). There are a number of well-known articles on Lewinian action research which, although rather technical and specialized, may be of interest (see Corey 1953; Lewin 1946; Rapoport 1970; Sandford 1970). The literature on action research and critical theory is growing. Carr and Kemmis' (1986) *Becoming Critical* provides an extensive rationale for action research; Rex Gibson's (1986) *Critical Theory and Education* provides an excellent introduction, while Youngs' (1989) *A Critical Theory of Education* is more theoretical. Of much interest is the work of Stephen Kemmis. His articles on action research (Kemmis 1982, 1983) provide an excellent overview of the topic, and the revised *Action Research Planner* (Kemmis and McTaggart 1988) not only contains a step-by-step guide, but also has useful introductory essays on action research. The papers by Elliott (1981) and Ebbutt (1985) extend Kemmis' work, all of which are critiqued in a rather polemical article by Hopkins (1984a). Background reading on the teacher-researcher movement and its educational context is found in Stenhouse's (1975) *An Introduction to Curriculum Research and Development* and in John Elliott's (1991) *Action Research for Educational Change.*

CHAPTER 5

Developing a Focus

Engaging in classroom research is often initially an un-
nerving and occasionally threatening experience. Trying
anything new involves uncertainty, and this is particularly
true of teacher research. Increasingly, however, teachers are
regarding the 'researching of practice' as part of their
professional responsibilities. It is important therefore that
the fourth criterion mentioned in the previous chapter –
that of identifying and being committed to a topic for
classroom research which is stated in workable terms – is
adhered to. But even when this is the case, it is often
difficult to establish a precise focus for the enquiry. For
these reasons, I will in this chapter review some ways in
which teachers can develop a focus for classroom research,
establish research questions and engage in theorizing. In
short, this chapter deals with how to get started on
classroom research.

DEVELOPING A FOCUS

Teacher research does not necessarily start with the setting
of precise hypotheses! As Kemmis and McTaggart
(1981: 18) point out in their first edition of *The Action
Research Planner*:

You do not have to begin with a 'problem'. All you need is a general idea that something might be improved. Your general idea may stem from a promising new idea or the recognition that existing practice falls short of aspiration. In either case you must centre attention on:

- What is happening now?
- In what sense is this problematic?
- What can I do about it?

  General starting points will look like –

- I would like to improve the. . .
- Some people are unhappy about. . .
- What can I do to change the situation?
- I am perplexed by. . .
- . . . is a source of irritation. What can I do about it?
- I have an idea I would like to try out in my class.
- How can the experience of . . . be applied to. . .?
- Just what do I do with respect to. . .?

As you read the extract, no doubt certain ideas or topics for classroom research come to mind. These ideas may also relate to the priorities on the school's development plan, or to the school's aims or mission statement. It is worth taking a few minutes to jot down these ideas; don't worry about how well they are formed, at this stage it is more important to generate a list of topics from which one can work. Having produced a list, the next step is to evaluate the usefulness, viability and/or importance of the individual topic. There are a number of guidelines that can be of use here.

First, do not tackle issues that you cannot do anything about. For example, it may be impossible in the short or medium term to alter the banding or streaming system in your school or to change the textbook that you are using. Because you cannot do anything about it, either avoid the issue or rephrase it in a more solvable form. So, although you cannot change the textbook, it may be possible to experiment with different ways the text could be used as evidence in your classes.

Second, only take on, at least initially, small-scale and relatively limited topics. There are several reasons for this. It is important to build on success, and a small-scale project satisfactorily completed in a short space of time is reinforcing and encouraging. It is also very easy to underestimate the scale and amount of time a project will take. It is very discouraging to have found after the initial flush of enthusiasm that you have bitten off more than you can chew.

Third, choose a topic that is important to you or to your students, or one that you have to be involved with anyway in the course of your normal school activities. The topic that you focus on needs to be intrinsically motivating. If not, then again after the initial flush of enthusiasm and when the difficulties begin to build up, you will find that motivation will begin to evaporate.

Fourth, as far as possible try and work collaboratively on the focus of your classroom research. Professional partnerships, as is seen in the examples given in Chapters 2 and 6, are a powerful form of professional development and personal support. It is also a way of reducing the isolation that some teachers work in.

Finally, make connections between your classroom research work and the school's development plan priorities or the school's aims. Although there need not be a direct relationship, it is important to relate one's individual professional enquiry to whole school initiatives and the direction that the school is moving in.

In summary, then, when choosing a topic or focus for classroom research, make certain, at least initially, that it is viable, discrete, intrinsically interesting, involves collaboration and is related in some way to whole school concerns.

PERFORMANCE GAP

A growing body of research suggests: (1) there is often incongruence between a teacher's publicly declared philosophy or beliefs about education and how he or she behaves in the classroom; (2) there is often incongruence between the teacher's declared goals and objectives and the way in which the lesson is actually taught; and (3) there is often a discrepancy between a teacher's perceptions or account of a lesson, and the perceptions or account of other participants (e.g. pupils or observers) in the classroom (see Elbaz 1983). All of these discrepancies reflect a gap between behaviour and intention. The Ford Teaching Project also monitored the 'performance gap' between teachers' aspirations and their practice. These issues have more recently been commented on in contemporary reports on the state of primary education. The 'performance gap' therefore forms an important starting point for classroom research enquiries.

Dave Ebbutt (1985) writes about 'the performance gap' as follows:

> It is via the notion of a performance gap – a gap between espoused theory and theory in action – by which advocates of action research locate its niche as an appropriate mode of research in schools and classrooms. For instance Kemmis in his *Planner* uses this illustrative example:
>
>> There is a gap between the idea and the reality of inquiry teaching in my own classroom. Recognising this gap, I must develop a strategy of action if improvements in this kind of questioning are to be achieved. . .

If you now return to the list of possible classroom research topics that you have just generated, there is probably implicit in each of the topics a description of what is currently happening (that provides a basis for reflection) and an indication of some new action connected to the existing behaviour that will lead to improvement. So, for example, in the case studies in Chapter 2, the teachers identified an existing teaching behaviour and at the same time thought of ways in which this aspect of their teaching could be improved. It is this gap between what is and what could be that is an important source of motivation in classroom research by teachers.

Ebbutt (1985) also illustrates the notion of the performance gap by reference to the Open University course *Curriculum in Action* (1980). Here the course team are concerned with demonstrating the gap between the curriculum in action and the curriculum as intention. They do this by posing six simple questions:

1 What did the pupils actually do?
2 What were they learning?
3 How worthwhile was it?
4 What did I do?
5 What did I learn?
6 What do I intend to do now?

The concept of the performance gap is useful in refining your list of topics for classroom research. The identification of a gap between what is and what could be provides motivation for change and indicates a direction for improvement. Action leads out of existing behaviours towards a new articulated goal.

OPEN AND CLOSED QUESTIONS

Implicit in much of what I have written so far is the idea that a research focus emerges out of a teacher's critical reflection on classroom experience, which is then explored through the use of the classroom research procedures. In other words, both the formation and resolution of the research enquiry is grounded in the teacher's experience.

The formation of a research focus or question occurs within either an open or closed context. Open questions take as their starting point a teacher's critical reflection on his or her teaching. This reflection culminates in a decision to utilize classroom research techniques to understand more fully and then develop his or her teaching (using the techniques discussed in the following four chapters).

Sandra, in the first example in Chapter 2, started from an open position and developed hypotheses about her teaching by using classroom research procedures. Having identified a focus, Sandra then developed a plan for action. Similarly, the teachers working collaboratively in the third example in Chapter 2 also started from an open position. The open approach, then, is one where teachers engage in classroom research as a reflective activity. From this reflection they derive questions that can be researched and that subsequently provide a basis for action.

The closed approach deviates from the open in so far as many teachers have already identified a specific issue or hypothesis before engaging in classroom research. In this instance, their classroom research begins with the testing of a hypothesis or exploring a specific activity. So with the example of Ann in Chapter 2, who, having heard about a new teaching method that applied to her subject area, used classroom research to investigate the effectiveness of the approach. The science teachers working on teaching strategies in Key Stage 3, described in Chapter 11, also started with a specific or closed issue. In this case, the focus not only involved collaboration, but was also closely related to whole school concerns. In addition, their focus on teaching strategies had immediate and direct relevance for classroom practice.

In Chapter 11, there is a more extensive discussion of formulating evaluation questions. Although the purpose there is specifically evaluation, rather than classroom research more generally, the same principles apply. The *open* approach is characterized as:

- take a broad area of enquiry
- carry out the initial enquiry
- gradually focus the enquiry.

By way of contrast, the *closed* approach typically follows this sequence:

- take a specific issue

- derive research questions
- choose an appropriate methodology.

The difference between open and closed reflects the derivation of the focus. In the first instance, the hypothesis or question emerges as a result of critical reflection; in the second, it is a given, and the teacher having refined it proceeds to the enquiry. Both approaches reflect classroom research as it is defined in this book, because in both instances the research is controlled by the teacher for the purpose of improving practice. The contrast between open and closed questions or hypotheses can also be represented in diagrammatic form as in Fig. 5.1.

Type	Hypothesis
Open	Generating
Closed	Testing

Fig. 5.1

Dillon (1983) has produced a similar (if rather more academic) schema for conceptualizing 'problem formation'. He writes:

> Three existential levels of problem and three corresponding psychological activities can be identified as forming part of those events which may be appropriately designated as problem finding. In existential terms, a problem can be existent, emergent or potential. An existent problem has fully-developed being and appearance in the phenomenological field of events facing the observer. In psychological terms, the problem is evident and the observer perceives, recognizes, identifies it. At a second, less developed level an emergent problem exists which is implicit rather than evident. After probing the data – nosing about in the field of events, so to speak – the observer discovers or 'finds it'. At a still less developed level, a potential

problem exists. No problem in an ontological sense exists *qua* problem, but constituent elements are present, striking the observer as an inchoate problem. By combining these and other elements in some way, the observer creates, produces or invents a problem. These descriptive terms relate the existential and psychological dimensions of problem finding activity at three levels, as follows [see Fig. 5.2].

My purpose of going into such detail about developing research questions, or what others call 'problem formation', is simply to legitimize the position of teachers who want to engage in classroom research just to find out about their teaching. Classroom research is not solely about exploring specific 'problems' or testing explicit hypotheses. It is appropriate for teachers to use classroom research as a means of critically reflecting on their teaching and developing hypotheses about it.

FORMULATING HYPOTHESES

Whether or not teachers are initially involved in open or closed problems, they will have to formulate hypotheses or questions at some stage. As I suggested in Chapter 4, the teacher-researcher, either as an individual or as a member of a group, needs to define his or her problem clearly, for it is this definition that determines what data are collected and analysed. It is inevitable that our observations tend to be theory-laden, so consequently it is important to formulate as explicitly as one can the hypotheses that are being tested or the research questions one wishes to explore. If, for example, a group of teachers are concerned about the problem of initiating classroom discussion, they may first hypothesize that asking more open-ended questions would encourage freer responses; a number of different hypotheses could be developed and tested around this contingency. The hypotheses, however, need to be extremely clear and

PROBLEM LEVEL (existential/psychological)	PROBLEM ————	———— ACTIVITY ————	———— SOLUTION
1. existing/evident	. . . as problematic	Perceiving the situation (RECOGNITION)	. . . as resolved
2. emergent/implicit	. . . for elements of a problem	Probing the data (DISCOVERY)	. . . for elements of a solution
3. potential/inchoate	. . . a defined problem	Producing the problem-event (INVENTION)	. . . a defined solution

Fig. 5.2 A conceptual scheme for comparing levels of problem finding and solving.

precise. Because there are so many variables in the complex art of teaching, even a carefully worded hypothesis can sometimes only be reported as tentative and provisional. Pring (1978) gives some examples of classroom research hypotheses taken from the Ford Teaching project:

> In order to cut out 'the guessing game' and move from a formal to an informal pattern, teachers may have to refrain from the following acts:
>
> 1 Changing Topic
> Hypothesis. When teachers change the topic under discussion, they may prevent pupils from expressing and developing their own ideas, since pupils tend to interpret such interventions as attempts to get con- formity to a particular line of reasoning.
>
> 2 Positive Reinforcers
> Hypothesis. Utterances like 'good', 'interesting', 'right', in response to ideas expressed can prevent the expression and discussion of alternative ideas, since pupils tend to interpret them as attempts to legitimate the development of some ideas rather than others.

Following Popper's answer to the problem of induction (see Magee 1973: Ch. 2), it is more appropriate to formulate hypotheses as unambiguously as we can, so as to expose them as clearly as possible to refutation. For as Popper pointed out, although empirical generalizations are in principle not verifiable, they are falsifiable and, conse- quently, they can be tested by systematic attempts to refute them.

THEORY AND THEORIZING

Now a word about theory. So far, I have used the word in two distinct senses. The first refers to a set of personal assumptions, beliefs or presuppositions that individuals hold. Our view of the world, our individual construction of reality is at one level essentially theoretical. The second use of the word is in the more traditional or 'grand' sense, where theory refers to a coherent set of assumptions which purport to explain, predict and be used as a guide to practice. This is the sense in which the word was used when Ann, in the case study in Chapter 2, turned to theory in order to inform her classroom research problem.

Unfortunately, as I have hinted before and as has been clearly demonstrated by Pring (1978) and Stenhouse (1979), all too often educational theory in this second sense is not all that useful in telling us in a practical way how to behave in the classroom. In many instances, the gap between theory and practice is so large that it prevents any useful connection. This occurs because our theories are often not specific enough, or the propositions they contain are not easily generalized to individual situations. This, of course, is an unsatisfactory situation, and one that argues for a different approach to educational theory.

A viable alternative is to theorize about practice, and theorizing is a third way in which we can understand theory. Theorizing approaches theory through practice (the reverse of grand theory, which goes from theory to practice), much in the same way as the hypotheses, assumptions and constructs we develop from classroom research procedures emerge from data gathered from actual classroom experiences. The discussion of grounded theory in Chapter 9 illustrates how theory can be generated from data gathered in a substantive situation. When we are engaged in classroom research, we can be said to be engaged in educational theorizing because we are reflecting systematically and critically on practice. As Richard Pring (1978: 244–5) writes:

> Such systematic and critical examination will involve philosophizing, appealing to evidence, reference to . . . theories. But there is no reason for saying that it will add up to a theory. [Classroom research is about] helping the practitioner to theorize, i.e. think more

systematically, critically and intelligently about his or her practice.

You will remember that Stenhouse (1975) in his discussion of the teacher-researcher illustrates this attitude when he suggested that the teacher, instead of accepting uncritically what a particular theory claims, implements it in the form of a working hypothesis or curriculum proposal. This thought captures two of the fundamental aspects of what Donald Schon (1983) has called the 'reflective practitioner'. In educational terms, such professional teachers (a) stand in control of knowledge rather than being subservient to it and (b) by doing this they are engaged in the process of theorizing and achieving self-knowledge.

The idea of 'self-knowledge' is an important one in this context. It refers to the individual internalization of ideas that empowers the person. It refers to those moments of clarity and power that occur when we understand a concept and see how we can use it in our personal or professional lives. It is an exciting and exhilarating moment and one which, for teachers and pupils alike, is too rare in our schools. This, as I understand it, is the basis of Polyani's (1962) writing on *Personal Knowledge*. Personal knowledge is that which is mediated through subjective experience and subsequently owned by the individual. The most pertinent feature of Polyani's work is the concept of tacit knowledge, the knowledge we cannot articulate. He suggests that we know a great deal more than we can put into words, and that we sense and understand more than we can describe or explain. An aspiration of the approach to classroom research adopted in this book is for teachers to gain more clarity on their 'tacit knowledge' and to incorporate this in their teaching.

Walt Whitman (1855/1959) captures a similar thought in this evocative passage from *Leaves of Grass*:

> You shall no longer take things at second or third hand. . . nor look through the eyes of the dead . . . nor feed on the spectres in books,

You shall not look through my eyes either, nor take
things from me,
You shall listen to all sides and filter them from
yourself.

In this chapter, I have discussed the challenges involved
in developing a focus for classroom research by teachers. I
have been at pains to point out that the focus of an enquiry
can be either open or closed in so far as the teacher is
engaged in hypothesis generation or testing. I have also
pointed to some ways in which the focus of classroom
research can be clarified and made more specific, and linked
the whole discussion to a notion of theorizing and self-
knowledge. The underlying theme is that through developing a focus for their research, teachers gain more control
over their professional lives.

The advice in this chapter obviously applies to both
teachers working alone or in collaboration. For reasons
already rehearsed in previous chapters, I believe that
collaborative efforts at teacher research are to be preferred.
Talking to others, for example, is an excellent way of
clarifying the focus of a research enquiry. In the next three
chapters, we discuss practical ways in which data about the
focus of a classroom research enquiry can be gathered.

FURTHER READING

The third edition of *The Action Research Planner* by
Stephen Kemmis and Robin McTaggart (1988) contains
detailed and helpful advice on 'finding a theme' for classroom research. Other helpful sources for 'getting started'
are Judith Bell's (1993) *Doing Your Research Project*
(Second Edition) and Jean McNiff's (1988) *Action Research:
Principles and Practice*. More specific foci for classroom
research enquiries are comprehensively illustrated in Good
and Brophy's (1984) *Looking in Classrooms*. For a dis-

cussion of hypothesis generation, it is useful to look at some of the Ford Teaching Project materials (see Elliott 1976). The article by Dillon (1983) on problem finding is very informative. Bryan Magee's (1973) monograph on Popper is a paragon of clarity and neatly summarizes Popper's solution to the problem of induction. Donald Schon's (1983) *The Reflective Practitioner*, although not specifically about education, echoes many of the themes of this book, particularly in regard to how professionals develop and learn through reflection and action.

CHAPTER 6

Principles of Classroom Observation

Observation plays a crucial role not only in classroom research, but also more generally in supporting the professional growth of teachers and in the process of school development. In my experience, it seems to be the pivotal activity that links together reflection for the individual teacher and collaborative enquiry for pairs or groups of teachers. It also encourages the development of a language for talking about teaching and provides a means for working on developmental priorities for the staff as a whole. This chapter is therefore of central importance. I begin by outlining five criteria crucial to the successful practice of classroom observation, then describe the generic three-stage cycle of classroom observation and its specific application to partnership teaching. In discussing the principles underlying observation, the emphasis is not just on classroom research, but also more generally on teacher and school development. The following chapter is devoted to a description of four methods of undertaking classroom observation: *open, focused, structured* and *systematic* observation.

KEY FEATURES OF CLASSROOM OBSERVATION

Although I believe that in general classroom observation is a 'good thing', there are a number of specific skills associated with it which, if not acquired, can have disastrous results for the morale of individuals and the whole staff. The main problem, it seems to me, is that we jump too quickly to conclusions about the behaviour of others. As I note in Chapter 9, the philosopher Karl Popper claims that, 'observations . . . are [always] interpretations in the light of theories (Magee 1973: 107). Although we constantly need to use our personal theories to construct our worlds (and without doing so would not survive long in the classroom!), this uniquely human intuition is not the greatest asset during classroom observation. Moving to judgement too quickly is one of the main characteristics of poor observation. There are at least five key features of classroom observation that need to characterize our approach if the process is to lead to professional growth.

Joint planning

A joint planning meeting is of crucial importance, especially if it precedes the first in a series of observations. There is a need to establish at the outset a climate of trust between observer and observed, to agree on a focus that both regard as worthwhile, to discuss the context of the lesson, to sort out the 'ground rules' – time and place of the observation, where to sit, how to interact with the pupils, how long to spend in the classroom, etc. The more specific and focused the observation, the more there is a need for joint planning. Once the observer and the observed become familiar with each other's style and the roles are reversed, then the time spent in the initial meeting can be reduced. It may also be possible during an on-going cycle of observations to combine feedback and planning meetings.

Focus

There are two broad ways of categorizing the focus of classroom observation activities: general or specific. The terms are self-explanatory: the former indicating an approach where 'everything counts' and therefore could be commented on; and the latter where the observation is confined to a particular or well-defined classroom activity or teaching practice. When the focus is broad, the more likely it is that the observer, who having no criteria to turn to, will rely on 'subjective' judgements to interpret what is going on in the classroom. Although these judgements may be perfectly valid, they most probably will be of little use to the teacher being observed unless the basis for them has been discussed and agreed on in advance. The danger in this situation is that the teacher being observed is subject to a series of 'mini-judgements' on his or her teaching that tell you more about the educational values of the observer than the teacher whose classroom practice is under scrutiny. The more specific and more negotiated the focus of the classroom observation, the more likely it is that the 'data' so gathered will be useful for developmental purposes. If the focus for classroom observation relates to the development plan, then the observation could contribute both to teacher and school development.

Establishing criteria

The contribution of classroom observation to professional development is greatly enhanced if, during the initial discussion, criteria for the observation are established. I remember vividly during an interview on our evaluation of the 'School Teacher Appraisal' project, asking an appraiser, the head of a primary school, what criteria she used when observing her colleagues. 'We don't use checklists in this school', she replied angrily. 'Come on', I said, 'What were you looking for when you went into the classroom?' 'Oh', she said, 'Were the children smiling and engaged in their work? Was the classroom environment attractive? Was the work they were doing appropriate for their ability?', and so on. Before too long she had given me a fairly sophisticated description of 'good primary practice'. What a pity I thought that the staff of that primary school had not had that discussion before the start of the appraisal process. Criteria are nothing to be frightened of, particularly if they are negotiated and agreed *before* the start of an observation. It may be helpful for the staff as a whole to agree and develop criteria on a particular classroom observation before the cycle of observation begins. It is also important that such criteria are subject to ongoing review as those involved refine their definitions of good practice. When viewed in this way, the discussion of criteria can act as a 'road map' for development as well as providing standards by which to discuss the outcomes of an observation.

Observation skills

There are three main 'skills' involved here. The first is guarding against the natural tendency to move too quickly into judgement. This can be achieved to some extent, as we have seen already, by having a clear focus for the observation and agreeing the ground rules beforehand. Secondly, there are the interpersonal skills involved when 'invading another person's space'; this includes creating a sense of trust and being supportive in situations where the other person may feel threatened. The third skill area is more technical. It is knowing how to design schedules that will allow the observer to gather appropriate information on classroom movement or transactions, or of knowing which are the most appropriate checklists or *aide-mémoires* to use in a particular situation. This latter point is especially important, as one obviously wishes to avoid having the values underlying an observation schedule imposing themselves on the outcomes of the feedback discussion.

Feedback

The benefits of classroom observation will only be realized if appropriate feedback is given. Put another way, poor feedback is characterized by being rushed, judgemental, one-way and impressionistic. As has already been implied, feedback appears to work best if:

- it is given within 24 hours of the observation,
- it is based on careful and systematic recording,
- it is based on factual data,
- the factual data are interpreted with reference to known and agreed criteria,
- the interpretation comes in the first instance from the teacher who has been observed,
- it is given as part of a two-way discussion, and
- it leads to the development of strategies for building on what has been learnt.

THE THREE-PHASE OBSERVATION CYCLE

These key features lay the basis for a professional development approach to classroom observation. The 'three-phase observation cycle', originally called 'clinical supervision', was initially developed in North America as a method of supervising student teachers, but it is well suited for use in classroom research situations.

The three essential phases of this classroom observation process are a planning meeting, the classroom observation itself and a feedback discussion. The *planning meeting* provides the observer and teacher with an opportunity to reflect on the proposed lesson, and this leads to a mutual decision to collect observational data on an aspect of the teacher's classroom practice. During the *classroom observation* phase, the observer observes the teacher in the classroom and collects objective data on that aspect of the teaching or learning they agreed upon earlier. It is during the *feedback discussion* that the observer and teacher share the information gathered during the observation, decide on appropriate action, agree a record of the discussion, and often plan another round of observation. An outline of the process is given in Fig. 6.1. It is important to realize that to be effective, all three phases of the process need to be gone through systematically.

There are a number of principles that are important to consider in this approach to classroom observation. First, the climate of interaction between teacher and observer needs to be non-threatening, helping and one of mutual trust. Second, the focus of the activity should be on improving classroom practice and the reinforcing of successful strategies, rather than on criticism of unsuccessful patterns of behaviour, or changing the teacher's personality. Third, the process depends on the collection and use of objective observational data, not unsubstantiated value judgements. Fourth, teachers are encouraged to make inferences about their teaching from the data, and to use the data to construct 'hypotheses' that can be tested out in the

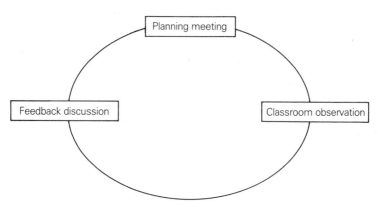

Fig. 6.1 The three-phase observation cycle.

future. Next, each cycle of observation is part of an ongoing process that builds on the other. Finally, both observer and teacher are engaged in a mutual process of professional development that can lead to improvement in teaching and observational skills for both. In all these ways, classroom observation can support both specific purposes, as well as the more general aspirations of teacher and school development.

An example of the three-phase approach to classroom observation is given by Marsha and George.

Marsha had already observed several of George's year 8 History classes. During a planning conference, they went over George's lesson plan. George identified his objectives, one of which was to involve as many pupils as possible in discussing a particular historical event. They decided to focus the observation on the type of questions George asked, and the pupils' responses. Marsha suggested she use a seating plan on which to 'tally' the voluntary and solicited comments from the pupils. George agreed and also requested that she jot down his questions verbatim.

During the lesson, Marsha recorded information for the twenty minutes George had planned for the discussion. Afterwards, as they went over the data, patterns began to emerge. George noticed that, although the discussion had been lively, only twelve out of the twenty-eight pupils had participated (he had thought during the lesson that more were involved). Also, certain types of questions tended to elicit more complete responses.

They both decided that it might be useful if George sequenced his questions from factual types (to establish a common knowledge base) to more open-ended, opinion questions. Also, now that he knew which pupils were reticent, George would attempt to involve them more in class discussions. Marsha suggested a couple of techniques that worked for her, and George was excited about trying them out. The feedback conference ended with both agreeing to use the same observation focus in the near future to compare the results of George's new strategies.

PARTNERSHIP OBSERVATION

The three-phase cycle provides a general framework for classroom observation which is particularly relevant to 'partnership' teaching or collaborative observation. I try to encourage teachers to engage in classroom research in pairs or small groups for a number of reasons. Among them is the emotional support they gain from each other, particularly as this activity is initially threatening. It is now fairly well established that teachers learn best from other teachers, and take criticism most easily from this source. It is ideal if teachers in cross-hierarchical groups can act as observers for each other, and this mutual exchange of roles quickly breaks down barriers which otherwise may be monolithic.

The observer in the partnership can play any number of differing roles. He or she can observe a lesson in general, focus on specific aspects of the teaching and talk to pupils all during one observation period. This lightens the teacher's problem of analysis and tends to increase the objectivity of the data gathered. In addition, the observer may also be able to note incidents that the teacher would ordinarily miss.

Colleagues involved in the University of Cambridge Institute of Education and Bedfordshire Education Service 'Developing Successful Learning Project' have been evolving an approach to classroom observation that emphasizes the partnership role. The following description is taken from their work.

This approach to partnership observation assumes that:

- all teachers can develop their practice, and
- all students can learn successfully.

It is based on the following principles:

- practice can only be improved in the contexts in which it normally occurs, and
- individuals need the support of colleagues as they seek to develop their practice.

The central strategy is to create partnerships of teachers who are committed to helping one another develop their classroom practice. These partnerships usually involve two or three colleagues who, for the purposes of this work, regard one another as equals. A partner must be somebody with whom you can work comfortably.

Before the observation, a number of issues have to be considered and decisions made by the partners:

- the role of the observer in the classroom,
- the confidentiality of discussions,
- commitment to the programme,
- date/time place of *observation*,
- date/time place of *review* – this should be set as near to the observation as possible (within 24 hours); the place must be one without interruptions, on or off site, and needs to be non-threatening; it is best to allow a minimum of 40 minutes for the review,
- how often observation is to take place – this is dependent on the timetable and the availability of cover,
- which classes and lessons are to be observed,
- whether this is to be a focused or unfocused observation, and
- methods of observation to be used.

During the observation, the observer should only record what is seen or heard and not be judgemental or intrusive. Time should also be found for one or two minutes of positive discussion at the end of the observation period. This will allow the observed teacher to release any tension that may have developed during the lesson. The observer may also give the class teacher a copy of the observation notes.

During the review discussion, feedback should be non-threatening, supportive and based on the information gathered during the observation. *Target setting* evolves from feedback, and once this has been given it is time to identify one area of learning to be developed. Targets must be realistic and attainable within the designated time-span. This does not, however, preclude the developments continuing over an extended period. If successful, these changes often become an integral part of effective class teaching, thus enhancing the learning experience of students.

Action planning for development is based on the answers to a series of questions that need to be addressed before modifying teaching practice:

- What do I want to achieve?
- How am I going to achieve this?
- How will this improve the quality of learning?
- How will this development be evaluated?
- Will I involve the pupils in the process of monitoring and evaluation?
- Are there adequate resources to implement the proposed development?

If, after carrying out the *action plan,* the outcomes were not successful, do not be discouraged! Try to discover why. This is where assistance and advice from a 'third person' could be invaluable. Perhaps you were too ambitious in your objectives; if so, return to *target setting.* If the objective was realistic, it may have been the way in which it was developed in the class; if this was the case, return to the *action plan.* If the outcomes were successful, why were they? Always reflect on practice. The partnership may now wish to continue with the original target, or a new target may be set.

Examples from the work of the 'Developing Successful Learning Project' have already been given in Chapter 2. This further example of partnership observation, prepared by Pamela Hughes of Sharnbrook Upper School, focuses on involving students in the observation process.

This classroom project placed particular emphasis on the idea of student involvement. There are 29 students in the class. The project included the following steps:

1 Initially the students in the two classes involved were given letters to take home, to explain their involvement and to give parents an opportunity to contact us if they wished.
2 The students, working in groups, discussed and then listed things which (a) helped their learning and (b) hindered their learning within the class. (This took 10 minutes in one class and 30 in the other where it was used as an oral exercise.)
3 After the observation, the students in my class were very keen to be involved further. They knew that the focus would be evaluating group work, but they did not know the specific areas.

We discussed ways of evaluating our learning, but not in those terms! The outcomes, from the students, were recorded by further observation, videotaping and by questionnaire (testing was not mentioned). I explained that I had already designed a questionnaire. Somebody asked if the class could compile their own – we debated time, costs, what it would include, how to go about it, etc.

I decided to let them try during the following lesson. I was able to do this because they were year 9 and the task was suitable for an English lesson. I think this would have been more difficult to organize in other areas of the curriculum. They were also keen to video the lesson and one student was made responsible for setting it up in the corner of the room before the beginning of the lesson.

I began to think of my *action plan* when they undertook the task, i.e. using the board for key points and ensuring a better mix within groups.

The Lesson

The video   It was difficult to decide where to focus as we did not want it to be intrusive. The students decided that they would focus the camera on one side of the room and that half-way through a designated person would change its direction. The lesson followed afternoon registration and so there was no difficulty in setting the camera up prior to the class arriving.

The observation   This was unscheduled. We were just about to begin the lesson when a member of the class asked if one of them could observe as the other teacher had. I 'thought on my feet' and could not see any objection. I asked for a volunteer and chose the first hand that shot up. I knew that I did not have time to explain about how to do observation, so placed him in a position from where he could see most of the class and told him to write down anything that he thought might be affecting our learning. This would by nature be judgemental and for 'my eyes only'.

The task   The aim was for each group to produce a question-naire which would be used by a group, not an individual. Whole class discussion (using board for key points), followed by paired friendship groups. Further brainstorming as a class, followed by each pair joining another. I chose the groupings.

Follow-up

I used the student observation notes and the video with my teaching partner, Christine. We were both surprised at the candid nature of the observation notes. Groups of students have also seen extracts from the video (during lunch-times) and this has led to further discussion. One 'spin-off' from the student involvement has been greater tolerance of individuals within the class and the building of a more positive class identity.

Notes Made by the Class Member

(The comments in brackets have been added by Pamela Hughes.)

Beginning of lesson: everybody is chatting quietly. Then group task is explained. Groups are scattered around the room. (Group task in pairs.)

Same groups (pairs) as they are sitting in. They begin the group discussion. One pair messing around.

Everybody works with somebody of the same sex.

Groups talking.

People at the back of the class are working more than the people towards the front.

Another member of staff enters – pupils cease to work and then get back to what they were doing before they entered.

Class discussion

Most people are contributing to the questions.

Some people had very good questions.

Some doodling in their notebooks while class discussion.

Nobody talked between themselves during this part of class discussion.

A couple of people are chewing pencils, pens.

Some people seem to be getting bored.

Groups combine

People only joined in a mixed group when there was no other choice.

Once the groups had been rearranged there was new discussion.

People who did not want to really work together in groups are working better than groups made up of just friends.

The people working best are the people with the camera
   directed towards them.
Most of the groups seem to have forgotten about the camera.
People who are messing around at the beginning seem to
   have calmed down a bit.

When the camera was moved for a second time people who
   had been fairly quiet up until now suddenly started
   moving and talking.
The people who are not in the picture now relax and start
   playing the fool to the camera. (I collated the group tasks –
   some had not finished. Those who finished quickly began
   designing the layout.)

Quick response from all to correct teacher. (I cannot remember what this was – it may have been homework.)

Bell goes, chattering began and people started to pack away,
   but Mrs Hughes stopped them straight away.

   As this example demonstrates, classroom observation
can provide powerful insights into classroom practice, as
well as being a means of professional development and a
major tool for the classroom researcher. In this chapter, I
have attempted to describe some of the main principles
involved in doing classroom observation as well as providing a series of examples which hopefully give a feel of the
method in practice. I have emphasized the partnership
approach to observation because I feel that it is here where
the link between teacher and school development lies,
especially if the focus of the observation is related to whole
school issues. In the following chapter, we look more
closely at the methods available to the classroom observer
committed to enhancing classroom practice.

FURTHER READING

The 'clinical supervision' approach to classroom observation, on which this three-phase approach was based, is

described in a practical way by Acheson and Gall (1980) in their *Techniques in the Clinical Supervision of Teachers*. The other classic texts on clinical supervision are by Goldhammer *et al.* (1980) and Cogan (1973). The work of Jean Rudduck contains a number of examples of teachers in partnership (Rudduck 1982, 1991; Rudduck and Sigsworth 1985). Colin Hook's (1981) *Studying Classrooms* contains a detailed discussion of the place of classroom observation in teacher research, and Judith Bell's (1993) helpful book on research in general contains a rationale for a more traditional approach to classroom observation.

> ## CHAPTER 7

Methods of Observation in Classroom Research

Within the general framework of the three-phase classroom observation or partnership teaching approach, there is no one best method to use. When teachers observe each other teach, all they often require are simple ways of gathering information on basic topics, such as questioning techniques, on- or off-task behaviour, and classroom management. It is usually preferable for teachers to devise their own observation schedules, to invent them for a specific purpose. By doing this, there is usually more ownership developed over the subject of the observation and a better fit between the focus of the observation and the data-gathering method.

Before devising the observation checklist, it is often useful to ask some organizing questions in order to clarify the purpose of the observation. These questions are illustrative:

- What is the purpose of the observation?
- What is the focus of the observation?

- What teacher/student behaviours are important to observe?
- What data-gathering methods will best serve the purpose?
- How will the data be used?

These and similar questions should help the teachers involved clarify how easy it is to use the chosen approach, how much the observer looks at and how far the observer makes judgements.

The next step is to decide on the observation method. Although there are many approaches, it is possible to categorize them into four main groups. Each of them could involve the use of 'pencil and paper', audio- or video-recording. They are open observation, focused observation, structured observation and systematic observation.

OPEN OBSERVATION

In this approach, the observer literally uses a blank sheet of paper to record the lesson. The observer either notes down key points about the lesson or uses a personal form of shorthand for making a verbatim recording of classroom transactions. For example:

Teacher: Turn 2 p 46. Mary give us y. ans. to q. 1.
Mary: WW II was partly t. result of unresolved conflicts of WW I.
Teacher: That's 1 pt. of the ans. John give us y. ans.

The aim is usually to enable subsequent reconstruction of the lesson. A variation of this approach is to agree to record only those events that fit into certain broad categories or under certain headings, as shown in Fig. 7.1. A problem with this approach is that it is often unfocused and can lead to premature judgements. The best way to handle this approach is to make open recording as factual as possible and leave interpretation until a discussion after the

The observer should aim to record factual and descriptive information.
Teaching skills

(i) Presentation	
(ii) Indirect teaching	
(iii) Direct teaching	
(iv) Voice	
(v) Questioning strategies	
(vi) Feedback	
(vii) Subject matter	
(vii) Expectations	

Fig. 7.1 An example of open observation (from Bollington and Bradley 1990).

lesson. Because of its general nature, it is important to stick closely to each component of the three-phase cycle; otherwise what began as a mutual approach to observation could result in a one-way monologue!

In this extended example, Heather Lockhart describes how she went about observing her colleague Maureen's teaching.

Maureen has recently begun to doubt the effectiveness of her questioning techniques. She asked me to observe a review lesson on a 'Plants and Seeds' unit she had recently completed. We decided to concentrate on observing the effectiveness of her questioning techniques rather than the lesson content.

We also decided that I would be in the classroom strictly as an observer. I would not participate in the lesson in any way. We felt that, as many of the children in the room had been former students of mine and because I work with her class two periods every week, the children were familiar with me and comfortable in my presence. We also decided not to use a tape-recorder or videotape so that the children would not be inhibited by them. Maureen and I discussed the most effective way of monitoring and decided on a checklist. I made a checklist and showed it to Maureen. Maureen agreed that it should give us the information we needed.

I positioned myself in the room within the children's immediate sight but slightly separated from the group. As I was within the field of their vision, I would not be causing distraction through children turning to check to see what I was doing. By separating myself slightly from the group, I was implying that I was not participating in the lesson. Maureen reinforced this by telling the children that I was going to watch because I didn't believe that they knew anything about plants and seeds. As we had predicted, outside of an occasional quick glance or smile, the children tended to ignore my presence.

When we first sat down, Maureen allowed the class about a minute of 'wriggle time' before she began to speak. She quickly explained my presence, then went directly into the lesson. She began by giving the children 'fact' questions that they could answer directly from the pictures. The responses were slow to come. Few children volunteered to answer the first few questions. As Maureen continued with the 'fact' questions, the children became more excited and eager to answer.

Maureen then began to inject 'inference questions'. The children were experiencing such success with 'fact questions' that they experienced no trouble in making inferences from the pictures. She then interspersed questions which required the children to form opinions. Again, the children responded freely and confidently. The children began to get restless after about fifteen minutes and their attention began to wander. Maureen realized what was happening and quickly ended the lesson.

Looking at the checklist after the observation, my reactions to Maureen's questioning techniques were confirmed. The questions were asked clearly and concisely. The children had full understanding of the type of response that was being elicited. As they understood the questions, they were comfortable and eager to respond.

Maureen's interaction with the children was warm and caring. She listened carefully and respectfully to each response whether the response was correct or incorrect. She encouraged hesitant children by smiling at them, giving verbal encouragement or nodding while the child was speaking. She was careful to ensure that each child had the opportunity to respond at least once during the lesson.

I feel that Maureen has excellent questioning techniques. This includes the variety in the type of questions she asks, the manner in which she uses her voice, the positive reinforcement she employs, the pace of the lesson and the warmth she shows towards the children.

I feel that Maureen's main problem with questioning techniques is that she doesn't recognize her expertise in this area. I would suggest she tape the lessons that use intensive questioning methods and analyse the results for her own benefit.

FOCUSED OBSERVATION

When a pair of teachers have decided on a focus for an observation (e.g. questioning technique), they are often at a loss as to exactly what to look at or for. They may not know, for example, the range of higher-order/lower-order questions. In another situation, they may have decided to look at 'praise' in their classrooms, but when they think more about it they may have some difficulty in describing all the different possible forms of praise. Or again even with a phrase as commonplace as 'effective teaching', what exactly is it that we are looking for? In these situations, it may be helpful to draw on some external resources to help focus the observation. It may be that the teachers who were focusing on 'questioning' would find a form like that illustrated in Fig. 7.2 of some help; or the teachers

FORM 10.6 Questioning Techniques

USE: When teacher is asking class or group questions

PURPOSE: To see if teacher is following principles for good questioning practices

For each question, code the following categories:

Behaviour categories

A *Type of question asked*

1. Academic: Factual. Seeks specific correct response
2. Academic: Opinion. Seeks opinion on a complex issue where there is no clear-cut response
3. Non-academic: Question deals with personal, procedural, or disciplinary matters rather than curriculum

B *Type of response required*

1. Thought question. Student must reason through to a conclusion or explain something at length
2. Fact question. Student must provide fact(s) from memory
3. Choice question. Requires only a yes–no or either–or response

C *Selection of respondent*

1. Names child before asking question
2. Calls on volunteer (after asking question)
3. Calls on non-volunteer (after asking question)

D *Pause (after asking question)*

1. Paused a few seconds before calling on student

	A	B	C	D	E
			CODES		
1.	1	2	2	1	2
2.	1	2	2	1	2
3.	1	3	2	1	2
4.	1	2	2	1	2
5.	1	2	2	1	2
6.	1	3	2	1	2
7.	1	2	2	1	2
8.	2	1	2	1	1
9.	1	2	2	1	2
10.	1	2	2	1	2
11.	1	2	2	1	2
12.	1	2	2	1	2
13.					
14.					
15.					
16.					
17.					

2. Failed to pause before calling on student   18. _____
3. Not applicable; teacher named student before asking question   19. _____
   20. _____

E *Tone and manner in presenting question*   21. _____
   1. Question presented as challenge or stimulation   22. _____
   2. Question presented matter-of-factly   23. _____
   3. Question presented as threat or test   24. _____
   25. _____
   26. _____

Record any information relevant to the following: 27. _____
Multiple Questions. Tally the number of times the teacher: _II_   28. _____
1. Repeats or rephrases question before calling on anyone _O_   29. _____
2. Asks two or more questions at the same time _O_   30. _____

Sequence. Were questions integrated into an orderly sequence or   31. _____
did they seem to be random or unrelated?   32. _____
Teacher seemed to be following sequence given in manual   33. _____
(led up to next history unit).   No   34. _____
Did students themselves pose questions?   35. _____
   36. _____

Was there student–student interaction? How much?   *None*   37. _____
   38. _____
   39. _____
When appropriate, did the teacher redirect questions to several   40. _____
students or ask students to evaluate their own or others' responses?   *No*

Fig. 7.2 Questioning techniques (from Good and Brophy 1984).

Table 7.1 Guidelines for effective praise

Effective praise	Ineffective praise
1. Is delivered contingently	1. Is delivered randomly or unsystematically
2. Specifies the particulars of the accomplishment	2. Is restricted to global positive reactions
3. Shows spontaneity, variety and other signs of credibility; suggests clear attention to the student's accomplishment	3. Shows a bland uniformity that suggests a conditioned response made with minimal attention
4. Rewards attainment of specified performance criteria (which can include effort criteria, however)	4. Rewards mere participation, without consideration of performance processes or outcomes
5. Provides information to students about their competence or the value of their accomplishments	5. Provides no information at all or gives students information about their status
6. Orients students towards better appreciation of their own task-related behaviour and thinking about problem-solving	6. Orients students towards comparing themselves with others and thinking about competing
7. Uses students' own prior accomplishments as the context for describing present accomplishments	7. Uses the accomplishments of peers as the context for describing students' present accomplishments
8. Is given in recognition of noteworthy effort or success at difficult (for *this* student) tasks	8. Is given without regard to the effort expended or the meaning of the accomplishment
9. Attributes success to effort and ability, implying that similar successes can be expected in the future	9. Attributes success to ability alone or to external factors such as luck or low task difficulty
10. Fosters endogenous attributions (students believe that they expend effort on the task because they enjoy the task and/or want to develop task-relevant skills)	10. Fosters exogenous attributions (students believe that they expend effort on the task for external reasons – to please the teacher, win a competition or reward, etc.)
11. Focuses students' attention on their own task-relevant behaviour	11. Focuses students' attention on the teacher as an external authority figure who is manipulating them
12. Fosters appreciation of, and desirable attributions about, task-relevant behaviour after the process is completed	12. Intrudes into the ongoing process, distracting attention from task-relevant behaviour

Source: Reproduced with permission from Brophy (1981).

Table 7.2 What are the findings of the research on teaching effects?

A summary of the substantive findings from studies of teaching effects falls into three broad categories: time and curriculum, classroom management and instructional quality.

Time and Curriculum. Student achievement is influenced by the way time is allocated by teachers and used by students in classrooms. It follows that interventions which affect instructional time are likely to affect achievement. But time alone is not the measure of quality in teaching. At the very least, our conception of time in classrooms must include a dimension of curriculum. Curriculum most often shows up in studies of teaching as content covered and/or opportunity to learn. The most sophisticated form of this measure is 'academic learning time', i.e. the time students spend working successfully with content measured on the criterion achievement test. In thinking about instructional time, it is necessary to consider not only whether students are paying attention, but also what they are doing – solving work problems, answering comprehension questions, writing expository essays – and whether these 'pursuits' are related to the curriculum being tested. When alignment occurs, students achieve. In this sense, opportunity to learn is a fundamental condition for student achievement.

Classroom management. Whether students actually utilize their opportunities to learn depends in part upon how well teachers organize and manage classrooms. Central to this view of classroom order is a *work system* consisting of activities which organize students for working and rules and procedures which specify actions for routine events. The most important feature of the work system for a class is the *programmes of action* that defines the nature of order for particular segments of time and pulls students along specified paths. The teacher's role in management has at least three dimensions. First, they prepare in advance for how students as a group will be organized to accomplish work and what rules and procedures will govern movement and routine events. Secondly, successful teachers communicate their work systems clearly to students through explanations, written materials, rehearsals and sanction. Finally, successful teachers monitor classroom events to make sure that the work system is operating within reasonable limits and to notice early signs of potential disruptions.

Dimensions of instructional quality. Given equal emphases on content and orderly classrooms, differences in student achievement will result among classes from differences in the quality of instruction, i.e. the design of assignments, the clarity of explanations, the chances students have to practice, and the availability and accuracy of feedback. A complete picture of effective teaching must include, therefore, dimensions of instructional quality.

Classroom studies of teaching effects have generally supported a direct and structured approach to instruction. That is, students usually achieve more when a teacher:

1 Emphasizes academic goals, makes them explicit, and expects students to be able to master the curriculum.
2 Carefully organizes and sequences curriculum experiences.
3 Clearly explains and illustrates what students are to learn.
4 Frequently asks direct and specific questions to monitor students' progress and check their understanding.
5 Provides students with ample opportunity to practise, gives prompts and feedback to ensure success and correct mistakes, and allows students to practise a skill until it is overlearned or automatic.
6 Reviews regularly and holds students accountable for work.

From this perspective, a teacher promotes student learning by being active in planning and organizing instruction, explaining to students what they are to learn, arranging occasions for guided practice, monitoring progress, providing feedback, and otherwise helping students understand and accomplish work.

Source: Adapted from Doyle (1987: 93–6).

interested in praise may find the lists of effective and ineffective praise illuminating (see Table 7.1); similarly, the teachers who were discussing effective teaching may find the summary of research provided by Walter Doyle a useful starting point (see Table 7.2).

All of these forms, *aide-mémoires* and summaries of research can be of help as long as they are subject to the teacher's own judgement. Problems arise when the checklist controls the focus of the observation, or encourages the observer to become judgemental. As Lawrence Stenhouse (1975: 142) said in another context, such specifications are to be regarded as intelligent, not necessarily correct. They are there to help focus and refine the teacher's judgement, not supplant it. It should also go without saying that such 'prompts' should be agreed and negotiated beforehand. If the use of criteria are implied in the observation, then they also should be negotiated, shared and understood by all those involved.

STRUCTURED OBSERVATION

Although the *aide-mémoires* described in the previous section are helpful in some situations, often all that an observer requires is fairly simple information that can be collected by either using a *tally system* or a *diagram*. I call this approach 'structured observation'.

With a *tally system*, an observer puts down a tally or tick *every time* a particular event occurs, e.g. every time the teacher asks a question or gives praise. The resulting record is factual rather than judgemental and can be made more detailed by basing them on *aide-mémoires* such as those described earlier. The aim of a *diagram* is to produce a record of what happens in the classroom. It records in diagrammatic form a series of classroom interactions. This approach lends itself to a factual or a descriptive record. It should be noted that all of these approaches can fit a wide range of concerns. They can focus on aspects of the teacher's work, pupil–teacher interaction or the work of one or more pupils.

The following examples of structured observation involve both tally systems and diagrams. They were developed by teachers who were interested in gathering data on questioning techniques and on/off-task behaviour.

Observing questioning techniques

1 *Question distribution*: in Box 7.1 the circles represent pupils. When they answer a question, the number of the

Box 7.1

Box 7.2

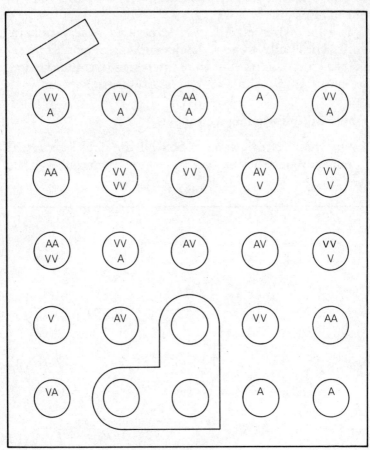

question is entered into their circle; blank circles indicate pupils who have not answered a question.

2 *Volunteered and solicited answers*: again in Box 7.2 the circles represent pupils. Use a 'V' for pupils who volunteer answers and an 'A' for those who are asked to answer. Placing a sub-letter beside the 'V' or 'A' will indicate the sequence of the questioning (e.g. V1, A2, V3, V4, A5, A6, etc.).

3 *Teacher response to questions answered*: indicate how

Box 7.3

QUESTION	RESPONSE				
	V	NV	+	0	−
1	✓		✓		
2	✓		✓		
3		✓	✓		
4	✓				✓
5		✓		✓	
6	✓		✓		
7	✓		✓		
8	✓			✓	
9		✓	✓		
10		✓		✓	
Totals	6	4	6	3	1

the teacher responds to answers by using the following abbreviations. Tally scores as in Box 7.3.

   V = verbal response
 NV = non-verbal response
   + = indicated positive response
   0 = indicated no response
   − = indicated negative response.

Observing on-task/off-task behaviours

- Identify, by scanning the classroom, all of the students who appear to be off-task every two minutes. Number

Box 7.4

each scan, using the same number for all pupils who appear to be off-task during that scan. For example, during scan 7, five pupils appeared to be off-task as in Box 7.4.

- Tally on-task/off-task behaviour: list in the off-task column, the number of pupils off-task at each scan (say every two minutes). Subtract the off-task from the class total to determine on-task pupils. Work out the percentages as in Box 7.5.

Box 7.5

SCAN	OFF-TASK			ON-TASK	
	Number	%		Number	%
1	4	16		21	84
2	6	24		19	76
3	1	4		24	96
4	0	0		25	100
5	3	12		22	88
6	3	12		22	88
7	6	24		19	76
8	5	20		20	80
9	4	16		21	84
10	4	16		21	84
Total	36			214	
Average		15			85

- Tally observable off-task behaviour by using the following code:

    1 talking not related to task assigned,
    2 doodling,
    3 daydreaming,
    4 wandering around,
    5 working at other tasks,
    6 physically bothering other pupils,
    7 attempting to draw attention,
    8 pencil-sharpener, fountain, washroom,
    9 other.

Box 7.6

STUDENT	SCAN										
	1	2	3	4	5	6	7	8	9	10	%
Jeroen	3	4				3		8			40
Jessica	2	2		3	3		4	2	3	2	80
Marloes	6	7			6	6		7			40
David		5	5			5	5		5		50
Dylan	1	1	1	8				8	1		70

This observation is easiest to do if you concentrate on a small number of pupils over an extended period of time, rather than trying to observe a whole class at once. During each scan (say every two minutes), observe the off-task behaviour and place the appropriate number in the space. If the student is on-task during the scan, the space is left blank as seen in Box 7.6.

SYSTEMATIC OBSERVATION

Although it may be preferable for teacher-researchers to devise their own observation scales, sometimes they may not have the time, or they may already be familiar with an existing coding scale previously invented. In this section, I will discuss a variety of coding scales that can be utilized in specific situations by teachers, and give a more detailed illustration of one interaction scale – the Flanders Inter-action Analysis Categories.

The research approach that relies entirely on the use of observation scales is known as 'systematic classroom observation'. The impetus for coding scales and checklists has come from North America where there is, and has been for some time, a concern for 'scientific' approaches to teaching (Gage 1978). But there is also a strong British tradition of systematic classroom observation; for example, the Oracle Project in primary education that was the first large-scale study of classroom interaction in Britain (Galton *et al.* 1980).

There are some potential problems in the use of coding or interaction scales. The first problem is that most scales were not designed for use by teachers. Their original intent was as research tools for analysing classrooms. Given the aspirations of this book, however, it is important to stress that these are tools teachers can use to enhance their practice. The teacher-researcher's orientation is always action.

The second difficulty is that each scale represents the author's concept of a situation. One is looking at classrooms through someone else's eyes: their purposes and perceptions could be very different from one's own. It is easy, therefore, to get trapped within the intentions of the researcher who designed the scale. Consequently, it is important for the teacher-researcher to match his or her needs closely to the intent and focus of the scale. In that way, the teacher-researcher can maintain control over the situation.

Thirdly, there is a heavy emphasis on quantitative methods in systematic observation. This often leads to a conflict between statistical rigour and analytical richness. In my opinion, this inevitably leads to abstraction rather than reflection on (or in) action. This approach often leads away from the classroom rather than into it. To misquote T. S. Eliot, systematic observers may well have the experience, but in so doing they are in danger of losing the meaning.

Because of the 'scientific' bias in this approach it is unsurprising to find that most coding scales available are American in origin. As Galton (1978) comments:

The obvious starting point for any classification of

interaction analysis systems must be *Mirrors for Behaviour* (Simon and Boyer, 1975). The current edition of this anthology contains some 200 observation schedules. Most are American and only two are British. In their collection the observation instruments are classified under eight main headings:

1 the subject of observation (teacher, pupil),
2 the setting under which the instrument is used (subject area),
3 the number of targets observed,
4 the coding unit used,
5 the collecting method employed,
6 the number of observers required,
7 the dimensions of the system (affective, cognitive), and
8 the uses reported by the author.

One of the problems with many of the American scales is that they are overly concerned with the formal teaching situation. British researchers have also been developing their own coding scales which, in general, stand in contrast to the American models. Galton (1978) comments again:

> A feature of British research has been the wide variety of different organisational contexts within which classroom observation has been carried out. Much criticism has been directed at American systems because they often seem appropriate only to the more formal type of teaching situation. One of the most interesting features of the British research is the emphasis on observation in informal settings at one extreme and the variety of schedules suitable for use in the microteaching setting for the purpose of evaluating performance in questioning and lecturing skills at the other.

These quotations from Galton (1978) are taken from his book *British Mirrors*, which is a collection of 41 classroom observation systems that are British in origin. The majority of these instruments are junior and secondary school oriented but some are specifically designed for infant or higher education settings. Their target is almost exclusively teachers and pupils, most require only one observer and they are almost exclusively concerned with descriptions of classroom practice. The four major foci of the instruments are: classroom climate, organizational learning, the management and control of routine activities, and knowledge content. In general, they are applicable across all curriculum areas.

One of the earliest coding systems is the Flanders Interaction Analysis Categories (FIAC). Although it may not necessarily be the most effective of the systems available, it is probably the best known. It is widely used and has influenced the design of many other category systems.

FIAC is based on ten analytical categories that reflects Flanders' conceptualization of teacher–pupil verbal interaction (see Table 7.3). Each of the categories has a number, but no scale is implied. In his book *Analysing Teaching Behaviour*, Flanders (1970) described the ten categories in detail, but for our purposes the descriptions given are sufficient. In order to help memorize the categories and make coding easier, one can shorten the descriptions of the categories as shown in Box 7.7. ·

The procedures for using the Flanders system are quite straightforward. Observers are first trained until they show a high level of agreement with other trained observers. Once they have been trained, they watch a lesson and apply the technique as follows using a coding sheet such as that illustrated in Fig. 7.3.

1 Every three seconds the observer writes down the category best describing the verbal behaviour of the teacher and class.
2 The numbers are written in sequence across the data sheet.

Table 7.3 Flanders Interaction Analysis Categories

Teacher talk

Indirect influence

1 *Accepts feeling*: accepts and clarifies the feeling tone of the student in a non-threatening manner. Feelings may be positive or negative. Predicting and recalling feelings are included

2 *Praises or encourages*: praises or encourages student action or behaviour. Jokes that release tension, not at the expense of another individual, nodding head or saying 'uh huh?' or 'go on' are included

3 *Accepts or uses ideas of student*: clarifying, building or developing ideas or suggestions by a student. As teacher brings more of his own ideas into play, shift to category 5

4 *Asks questions*: asking a question about content or procedure with the intent that a student answer

Direct influence

5 *Lectures*: giving facts or opinions about content or procedures, expressing his own idea; asking rhetorical questions

6 *Gives directions*: directions, commands or orders with which a student is expected to comply

7 *Criticizes or justifies authority*: statements, intended to change student behaviour from non-acceptable to acceptable pattern; bawling someone out; stating why the teacher is doing what he is doing, extreme self-reference

Student talk

8 *Student talk-response*: talk by students in response to teacher. Teacher initiates the contact or solicits student statement

9 *Student talk-initiation*: talk by students, which they initiate. If 'calling on' student is only to indicate who may talk next, observer must decide whether student wanted to talk. If he did, use this category

10 *Silence or confusion*: pauses, short periods of silence, and periods of confusion in which communication cannot be understood by the observer.

Source: Open University (1976).

Box 7.7

Teacher talk	1 2 3 4 5 6 7	accepts feelings praise accepts ideas question lecture command criticism
Pupil talk	8 9	solicited unsolicited
	10	silence

Source: Open University (1976).

3 Each line of the data sheet contains twenty squares, thus representing approximately one minute of time.

4 Separate 'episodes' can be identified by scribbled margin notes, and a new line commenced for a new 'episode'.

5 In a research project, the observer would have a pocket timer designed to give a signal every three seconds, thus reminding him or her to record a tally (a stop-watch or the second hand of a wristwatch can be used).

Two main advantages of the Flanders system are that it is fairly easy to learn and apply, and that the ten categories describe a number of behaviours which many would agree are important, such as the teacher's use of praise and criticism and the pupil's solicited and unsolicited talk. Also, the tallying of events every three seconds enables considerable information to be collected and analysed. There is usually a high agreement between trained observers.

On the other hand, much information is lost, especially non-verbal aspects of communication. In particular, some categories are too broad (e.g. category 4) and others discriminate insufficiently. For example, category 5 does not discriminate between giving information which is correct and that which is incorrect. Category 10 can represent both

School _____ Teacher _____

Class _____ Subject _____

Date _____ Observer _____

Lesson (1st, 2nd, etc.) _____

TALLY ACROSS

01																					
02																					
03																					
04																					
05																					
06																					
07																					
08																					
09																					
10																					
11																					
12																					
13																					
14																					
15																					
16																					
17																					
18																					
19																					
20																					
21																					
22																					
23																					
24																					
25																					
26																					
27																					
28																					
29																					
30																					

Fig. 7.3 FIAC lesson observation sheet (Open University 1976).

the silence achieved by an autocrat and the chaos which occurs when a teacher has lost control. Also, there are too few pupil categories, and it is difficult to use in informal classrooms, where two or more members may be talking at once.

For our purposes, FIAC is most appropriately used as a means for gathering classroom data that can then be used as a basis for action. So, for example, if after using FIAC a teacher discovered that he or she was talking too much, then that becomes an identifiable problem upon which action can be taken and monitored by classroom research procedures.

A simple example illustrates the first few seconds of an exchange occurring in the twelfth minute of a lesson.

The teacher tells children to look at a map on page 60 of their books and asks the name of the country coloured green. There is a short pause and then a child replied. The text of this exchange and the data sheet would look like that shown in Box 7.8.

Box 7.8

	Category number tallied by observer
Teacher: 'Look at the map on page 60'	6 (command)
Teacher: 'What is the country coloured green?'	4 (question)
three-second pause	10 (silence)
Pupil: 'I think it's Finland, but I'm not sure.'	8 (solicited pupil talk)

Data sheet entry
(minute 12 of the lesson)

12	6	4	10	8

Source: Open University (1976)

FURTHER READING

Rob Walker's (1985) *Doing Research* and Colin Hook's (1981) *Studying Classrooms* both contain exemplary and sound advice on methods of classroom observation that are sympathetic to the theme of this book. Walker and Adelman (1975) also provide useful information on classroom observation. Hitchcock and Hughes (1989), in their *Research and the Teacher*, provide extensive advice but from a more traditional perspective. Good and Brophy's (1984) *Looking in Classrooms* contains many schedules for assessing classroom behaviour; this book is an important resource for teacher-researchers, as it provides a range of material on teaching skills and ways of measuring their impact in the classroom. Sara Delamont's (1983) *Interaction in the Classroom* is a balanced and introductory account of the domain of classroom observation research. Paul Croll's (1986) *Systematic Classroom Observation* contains a fairly sustained argument for the centrality of systematic observation in quantitative research. This book also provides a detailed introduction to the large-scale *Oracle* and *One in Five* classroom interaction research studies. The approach taken in this book, however, tends to lead away from the classroom rather than into it, and Croll over-emphasizes, in my opinion, the distinction between teachers and researchers rather than the benefits of collaboration between them. In the same tradition, the two collections of classroom observation scales by Simon and Boyer (1975) and Galton (1978) are primary resources for teacher-researchers wanting examples of coding scales. Critiques of these various approaches to classroom interaction and observation are to be found in Sara Delamont's (1984) *Readings on Interaction in the Classroom* and Martin Hammersley's (1986) *Controversies in Classroom Research*.

▷ CHAPTER 8

Data Gathering

In this chapter, I discuss a variety of techniques other than observation that teachers can use to gather information about their teaching. I will observe a similar format in discussing each of the approaches: the technique will briefly be described, advantages and disadvantages will be considered, appropriate uses will be stated and an example of the technique in practice will be given. At the end of the chapter, I will present a taxonomy of teacher research methods.

The Ford Teaching Project (Elliott and Adelman 1976) in general, and the booklet *Ways of Doing Research in One's Own Classroom* (Bowen *et al.* n.d.) in particular, provided the inspiration for this chapter. The idea for the boxes illustrating the advantages/disadvantages of the data collection methods came from the appendix of *Ways of Doing Research in One's Own Classroom* and a number of the points made there are reproduced here verbatim. Also, all the methods of data collection mentioned below, with the exception of sociometry, were used by the Ford Teaching Project. Once again I am very grateful to the Ford Teaching Project for allowing me to use their material in this chapter.

Before describing these methods in more detail, two caveats have to be entered. The first is that describing the techniques individually may give a false impression of orderliness and discreteness. In practice, these techniques are more often than not used eclectically and in combination. Second, we need to remember the criteria established earlier which cautioned that the method employed should not be too demanding on the teacher's time.

FIELD NOTES

Keeping field notes is a way of reporting observations, reflections and reactions to classroom problems. Ideally, they should be written as soon as possible after a lesson, but can be based on impressionistic jottings made during a lesson. The greater the time-lapse between the event and recording it, the more difficult it becomes to reconstruct problems and responses accurately and retain conscious awareness of one's original thinking. Many teachers I know keep a notebook open on their desk or keep a space in their daybooks for jotting down notes as the lesson and the day progresses. Keeping a record in this way is not very time-consuming and provides surprisingly frank information that is built up over time. They also provide a fascinating biographical record of our development as teachers.

Field notes can be of a number of different types. They can be 'issue-oriented' in so far as the observations focus on a particular aspect of one's teaching or classroom behaviour and constitute an ongoing record. On the other hand, they can reflect general impressions of the classroom, its climate or incidental events. Field notes can also be used to provide case study material of a particular child. This information should be descriptive rather than speculative, so that a broad picture amenable to interpretation can be built up.

The main advantages and disadvantages of field notes are listed in point form in Box 8.1. Four uses of field notes in classroom research are:

- They can focus on a particular issue or teaching behaviour over a period of time.

Box 8.1

ADVANTAGES	DISADVANTAGES
• Very simple to keep; no outsider needed	• Need to fall back on aids such as question analysis sheets, tapes and transcripts for specific information
• Provide good ongoing record; used as a diary they give good continuity	• Conversation impossible to record by field notes
• First-hand information can be studied conveniently in teacher's own time	• Notebook works with small groups but not with a full class
• Acts as an *aide-mémoire*	• Initially time-consuming
• Helps to relate incidents, explore emerging trends	• Can be highly subjective
• Very useful if teacher intends to write a case study	

- They can reflect general impressions of the classroom and its climate.
- They can provide an ongoing description of an individual child that is amenable to interpretation and use in case study.
- They can record our development as teachers.

In this example Ian uses field notes to build up a picture of the work ethic in a low academic set of 12–13 year-olds.

I started making observations, keeping a note pad on the desk. I chose not to take a particular focus. After making initial observations on movement, posture and seating arrangements, and after some interviews of a general nature concerning the pupil's attitudes to the teaching of language and the organization into sets that the pupils had to submit to, a picture of the work ethic of a low academic set was gradually built up.

For each distinct activity that goes on in the English language lesson (story writing, grammar skills, etc.), the working environments and climates are different. In language work, for example, there is always an initial rush to complete *one* card – the minimum requirement. When this is completed, although another card is often collected, intensive work ceases and chatting about the weekend, with some desultory work, is the norm (the lesson is first period Monday). This ritualized behaviour has the function of reaffirming certain social groups, and talk is, interestingly enough, voluntarily kept to a quite quiet level. The various friendship groups have distinct topics of conversation which don't vary much over the year. Changes to the seating, which I have tried, cause a much higher level of noise. All the other English activities – each one has one lesson a week – have different structures and patterns of social interaction, attitudes and noise levels which have built up over time.

I noted that the pattern of work throughout the term – and the year – is affected by traditional school rituals. The arrangement of pupils into sets is reviewed at the end of each term and this ritual always influences work rate and conversation:

> *Girl*:   You 'eard about moving up yet, sir?
> *Teacher*:   No, I've been asked to make three recommendations to go up and down. Mr . . . will make the decision. [chorus of inquiries]
> *Girl*:   Shut up you – you're thick. If you move, it'll be down. I hope I move up – we do no work in 'ere. 'Alf of 'em can't even write (looking at the boys). (Cheers from boys)

The low status of the set is always a factor in the pupils' perceptions of their ability and in their attitude to work.

[This example is taken from a series of teacher-researcher reports on children's thinking in Hull et al. *(1985)*. At a later date, the teacher could have used notes like this as 'evidence' in discussions with his students about their progress and aspirations.]

AUDIOTAPE RECORDING

Audiotape recording is one of the most popular teacher research methods. Transcripts are excellent for those situations where teachers require a very specific and accurate record of a limited aspect of their teaching, or of a particular interaction, say between a specific teacher and child or between two children. An increasing number of teachers are using audiotape as one further way of gathering data to support other forms of assessment, albeit on an incidental basis. Also, simply playing back tapes of one's teaching can be very illuminating and provide useful starting points for further investigation. Having a tape deck in one's car is a great asset for doing this.

Playing back tapes or making transcripts can be very time-consuming and expensive, however, unless the method is used judiciously. The Ford Teaching Project teachers and staff were very enthusiastic about this method, but they did have secretarial support for making transcripts. Most teachers do not, and for that reason I advise against it as a broad-spectrum diagnostic tool.

On the practical side, the use of the tape-recorder requires some technical knowledge, so make certain you can use it before taking it into class and that the batteries are charged! It is important when recording to ensure that the microphone is picking up what is intended, and this also may require practice. Pupils often find the presence of a tape-recorder in the class disturbing and have to be introduced to the technique over time. Always check with the pupils and other teachers or adults that they do not mind you recording the conversation or discussion.

The main advantages and disadvantages of the audiotape

Box 8.2

ADVANTAGES	DISADVANTAGES
• Very successfully monitors all conversations within range of the recorder • Provides ample material with great ease • Versatility – can be transported or left with a group • Records personality developments • Can trace development of a group's activities • Can support classroom assessment	• Nothing visual – does not record silent activities • Transcription largely prohibitive because of expense and time involved • Masses of material may provide little relevant information • Can disturb pupils because of its novelty; can be inhibiting • Continuity can be disturbed by the practical problems of operating

recorder are listed in point form in Box 8.2. Three uses of the tape-recorder in classroom research are:

- as a general diagnostic tool for identifying aspects of one's teaching
- for providing detailed evidence on specific aspects of teaching through the use of transcripts, and
- as an additional source of evidence for classroom assessment.

In this example Val uses an audiotape-recorder as an aid to understanding children's thinking in relation to sketch maps in geography.

The class (of very bright 11 year-olds) was arranged in groups of four or five pupils and each group was given copies of the four maps and asked to discuss them and decide which they thought was 'best'. I only had access to one tape-recorder and was only able therefore to record one discussion. When I listened to the tape, I realized that discussion clearly had potential as a research tool and that this strategy for gaining access to pupils' critical thinking was worth repeating. Pupils were realistic in their criticisms and were to some extent impersonal. The discussion helped me to see what criteria they were using and how the range of their considerations might be extended.

In my next attempt . . . (there was only one tape-recorder available), there were several groups responding to the maps, so each group chose a leader and he or she gave a report to the class at the end of the discussion and it was the final reports that were taped. Some of the spontaneity of the original discussion was lost, but nevertheless some interesting points emerged.

It seemed that the brighter pupils were more methodical and precise in their criticism:

Simon: Our verdict on map 1 was that a ruler could have been used and some of the buildings had doors missing and that there wasn't any scale . . . title, key or north direction.

Map 3 – it's a drawing, it's not a map.

Map 4 – that's quite good, that's more of a map, they have got a key and direction and a suitable title.

Sarah: We thought map 1 wasn't very good because the writing is too small.

Map 3 wasn't very good – too artistic.

Valerie: Map 2 was the best because it showed all the roads and railways and bridges.

[This example is taken from a series of teacher-researcher reports on children's thinking in Hull *et al.* (1985). The teacher was subsequently able to use this information to revise the sketch maps; the discussions also helped her adapt her teaching style with more able pupils.]

PUPIL DIARIES

It is common practice in many schools for pupils to keep a daily log. This is also a quick way of obtaining information, as teachers normally check pupil diaries as a matter of course. Also, pupil diaries provide an interesting contrast to the field notes kept by the teacher on the same topic. Once the pupils have been taken into the teacher's confidence and are aware of the teacher's concern to research his or her teaching, then these diaries are an excellent way of obtaining honest feedback, particularly when the pupils retain the right to decide whether the teacher has access to the diary. The teacher can use pupil diaries as feedback on a particular teaching episode, or to gain an indication of the general class climate, or to assess the progress of an individual pupil. When pupils feel comfortable with the approach, they may feel free to write about other teachers and aspects of the school. Sometimes the ethical issues raised by this may be difficult to resolve, particularly when

Box 8.3

ADVANTAGES	DISADVANTAGES
• Provides feedback from pupil's perspective • Can be either focused on a specific training episode or related to the general classroom climate • Can be part of a lesson • Can help in identifying individual pupil problems • Involves pupil in improving the quality of the class • Provides a basis for triangulation	• May not be an established practice in the school • Difficult for younger children to record their thoughts and feelings • Pupils may be inhibited in discussing their feelings with the teacher • Pupil's accounts are obviously subjective • May raise ethical dilemmas

the use of pupil diaries is not commonplace in the school.

The main advantages and disadvantages of pupil diaries are listed in point form in Box 8.3. Three uses of pupil diaries in classroom research are:

- they provide a pupil perspective on a teaching episode
- they provide data on the general climate of the classroom, and
- they provide information for triangulation.

In this example Judy is using pupil diaries as part of her strategy for reorganizing her maths class.

I used the diaries mainly as immediate feedback for myself and as an aid in monitoring the daily progress of the students. The following are samples of information that I gathered from the various student diaries during a four-week period:

1. There were explanations as to why they hadn't completed a number of assignments for my substitute while I was at a convention.
2. Throughout the four weeks the students used the logs to tell me when they were having trouble with an assignment and to ask to see me the next day for help.
3. A number of students suggested that I put in a centre containing mazes and logic puzzles that they could go to when they had completed all their assignments.
4. Occasionally, a pupil would ask me to change their seating arrangement as they weren't able to work near a certain person.
5. Many of them began to use the log to establish a private conversation between us.
6. I used the logs to indicate when I was disappointed in a student's performance or behaviour and to question them about it. I found that they were more open since they weren't put on the spot in front of their classmates.
7. Some of them mentioned when they felt I had let the

noise level get too high or when they had been able to do more than usual because it had been exceptionally quiet.

8 They pointed out when they had wasted time waiting for me to get their books marked so they could finish off their corrections.

9 I found it especially helped me monitor the progress of my less assertive students.

10 The students would indicate when they felt I had given too heavy a workload for the week.

11 Students twice pointed out that they had come to me for assistance and I had been too busy to help them.

I felt that these logs were one of the most valuable aspects of my research project. They weren't always relevant to my actual research, but the personal contact I managed to establish with each of my students was of more importance to me than keeping them on target concerning their work in the maths programme.

INTERVIEWS

Interviewing in classroom research can take four forms: it can occur between teacher and pupil, observer and pupil, pupil and pupil and, occasionally, teacher and observer. This latter activity, however, normally occurs as a consequence of peer observation (see Chapters 6 and 7). Because teacher-pupil interviews are very time-consuming, it may be more profitable to devote that time to general classroom meetings, and only talk individually with pupils (for research purposes) when a specific instance warrants it. On the other hand, individual interviews are often very productive sources of information for a participant observer who wants to verify observations he or she has previously made. Like other researchers, however, I increasingly find group interviews with three or four students the most productive. Far from inhibiting each other, the individuals 'spark' themselves into sensitive and perceptive discussion. Pupil–pupil interviews can provide rich sources of data, particularly if the pupil interviewer keeps to an interview schedule prepared by the teacher. It is a good idea to tape-record these individual interviews for future reference, particularly if the encounters are relatively short.

Walker and Adelman (1975: 140) make a number of points about effective interviewing:

1 Be a sympathetic, interested and attentive listener, without taking an active conservative role; this is a way of conveying that you value and appreciate the child's opinion.

2 Be neutral with respect to subject matter. Do not express your own opinions either on the subjects being discussed by the children or on the children's ideas about these subjects, and be especially careful not to betray feelings of surprise or disapproval at what the child knows.

3 Your own sense of ease is also important. If you feel hesitant or hurried, the students will sense this feeling and behave accordingly.

4 The students may also be fearful that they will expose an attitude or idea that you don't think is correct. Reassure along the lines of 'Your opinions are important to me. All I want to know is what you think – this isn't a test and there isn't any one answer to the questions I want to ask.'

5 Specifically we suggest that you:

- phrase questions similarly each time,
- keep the outline of interview questions before you, and
- be prepared to reword a question if it is not understood or if the answer is vague and too general. Sometimes it is hard not to give an 'answer' to the question in the process of rewording it.

The main advantages and disadvantages of interviewing are listed in point form in Boxes 8.4 (a–c). Three uses of the interview in classroom research are:

- to focus on a specific aspect of teaching or classroom life in detail,

Box 8.4(a) Teacher/pupil (individually or in groups of three or four)

ADVANTAGES	DISADVANTAGES
• Teacher in direct contact with pupil • Pupil(s) familiar with teacher, therefore more at ease • Teacher able to seek information he or she wants directly and not through a ream of irrelevant information • Can be done in lesson time or outside the class • Can follow up problems immediately when they arise and get information while minds are still fresh	• Time-consuming • May be carried out with some form of recording equipment, with attendant disadvantages • Frequently difficult to get younger children to explain their thoughts and feelings

Box 8.4(b) Observer/pupil (individually or in groups of three or four)

ADVANTAGES	DISADVANTAGES
• Leaves teacher free as the interviewer discovers initial information from the pupil(s) • Pupil(s) frequently more candid with the outsider than with class teacher or teacher from within the school • Outsider is likely to be more objective • Outsider can focus the information provided along predetermined lines of investigation	• Pupil(s) unfamiliar with observer may be reluctant to divulge relevant information • Mutual uncertainty • If the teacher is the primary agent in the research, then he or she will get his or her information secondhand and subject to the biases of the interviewer • The whole set up is time-consuming as information goes from pupil(s) to interviewer to teacher • Difficult to obtain a skilled outsider

Box 8.4(c) Pupil/pupil

ADVANTAGES	DISADVANTAGES
• Pupils may be more candid with each other • Leaves teacher free • Can occur during lesson time • May produce unanticipated/ unusual perspectives	• Pupils may find the activity too unfamiliar • May encourage disruption • Has to be recorded and played to teacher

- teacher–pupil classroom discussion can provide general diagnostic information, and
- to improve the classroom climate.

This example contains extracts from a conversation between three year 9 students (S) at the Sanders Draper School, Havering, Mel Ainscow (MA), David Hargreaves (DHH) and myself (DH). Sanders Draper is involved in our 'Improving the Quality of Education for All' school improvement project. The purpose of the discussion was to assess how far the school's development priority 'Resource Based Learning' had affected students perceptions of the way they were taught and learned. We used this information in feedback to staff, who in turn incorporated it in their own developmental work. I have included such an extended illustration partly for its intrinsic interest, but also to show how classroom research can support whole school development and to illustrate the power of the group interview.

DH: What is it like to learn in this school?

S: It's changed now that we are able to use the library more, we are now using more visual/audio type stuff, videos, rather than just learning out of a textbook.

S: Also teachers tell you to get on with it, rather than them telling you what to do. You can come in here (the library), you find out all the information and you can say to a teacher I want to do this and that, and they say alright then.

S: Well we are more tending to get into things like, in maths for example, we tend to go into our own investigations where we can take a problem and we investigate it in our own way.

DH: Tell me a bit about how you actually find the information.

S: Well, if you find a book, look through the subject index, or there is a disk thing on the computer, its got all newspaper things, you put the disk in and you say what subjects you want to find out about, type it in and it comes up with all the different things in the subjects. You choose what you want. There is also an encyclopaedia list on the computer.

DH: What happens when you've done all this and got some information on the subject you are dealing with, say four or five bits of information – what do you do then?

S: We either make it into like a folder of work, put it into graphs, or sometimes we get the chance to make a play out of it, but there is still a certain amount of written work to record it all. Things like – they'll tell a certain amount of detail. Like in science they were telling us about disease and then we had to write a newspaper report about it, so used the pictures.

DH: What happens if you get into the situation where you find that one bit of information disagrees with another piece of information. How do you make a decision?

S: Usually you put both of the arguments, both for and against, or you decide which you think, but explain that there are other sides to the idea. Put down what you thought what was right and what was wrong. Put both sides down.

MA: That's quite demanding, do some students struggle with that?

S: It depends if you are looking through hundreds of encyclopaedias for the one thing you are looking for; otherwise you might as well watch it on the video if you are looking for something about the Third Reich, see if they've got a video about it. That's easier. There will always be people who work at different speeds, are capable of different things. When we do learning in our own way, then it is better because they are not trying to keep up with the top students in the class.

DHH: You have given me the impression that this new style of learning, your relationship with the teacher is different.

S: Well it is in some ways because there are some teachers who are sitting there and want to teach you everything on the line, but there are others who think it best for us to work down here (in the library).

DHH: But is it? Is it best for you?

S: Yes, I think it is. I prefer it anyway. You are at your own pace. Not like a teacher dictating to you and you just sitting there with your mouth open.

DH: Some people say that the real way to be taught is to write down lots of notes, do exercises from the book.

S: But the two ways compensate each other. You learn at your own pace and then answer the questions from the book. Then you remember it, take it in rather than just taking notes. You sort of construct it your own way. No real way of learning, different people find it easier to do different things, so I don't think anyone can say it is a lot better to work out of a textbook or it is a lot better to watch a video.

DHH: If I understand you correctly when you take notes, you are not really learning anything.

S: You learn about half of it but if you are in control of your own learning, you are doing it the way you want to do it, you actually want to learn about it, you are taking it in, and remembering more because you are doing it your way.

[*The students then showed us some examples of work.*]

MA: Who produced this?

S: I decided to do it on a computer at home, then it would be easier to read.

MA: So this in a sense summarizes all the research that you did, you've put it into your own words and made an information sheet.

S: Yes, that's what they said, do it like a magazine article, then it comes out in your own words. More likely to remember something that way.

DH: You have been in the school now for three years, do you think there has been a change in the way that teachers teach over those three years?

S: (Since the new Head arrived) the school has got more disciplined.

DH: More disciplined in the school, but at the same time a more open approach to teaching and learning?

S: Well we've been given the chance to like express ourselves, but because of that we've had to go by their rules.

DH: 'So there is a good response to this more open way.

S: Yes, you've got the responsibility of getting on with what you want to do, you've got to do it even if the teacher isn't watching you. It sort of works two ways, you respect the school rules and they'll respect you, they are trusting you to work on your own.

DHH: Somebody might say, from outside, that you might choose a very slow pace for yourself and the job of the teacher is to make you go at a faster pace. What do you say to that?

S: Well the teachers would like say to you, I don't think you have done enough work. If you have only done a couple of sentences of work for your whole project, they will like give you a detention, or a series of detentions, or something like that. That will teach you to work more rather than at a faster pace.

S: You will always have to do a certain amount of work, you will never give in one sheet of work for a project and it will be OK. That's never going to be told OK so that's your pace then.

DHH: So you are not going to get away with that sort of thing.

S: No.

DH: So that is an example of the rules on the one hand and the flexibility on the other.

S: Yes.

DHH: So it is tough in some ways but not in others.

S: Yes.

S: It's like the correct balance between lenience and strictness. No good coming in one day and doing a little work and then saying that's enough, then coming in the next day and doing nothing, you have to try to do as much work as possible on both days.

[*We were then shown another piece of work.*]

DHH: Did you change your mind on anything when you were writing.

S: Yeah I did actually. At first I thought the approach was all wrong and it should never be allowed. When I started researching into it and found out things, there are fors and against. I really decided that it was a matter of individuals really, so I put that in there. For and against, and then my own views.

DHH: It has a terrific ending to it. You went through the arguments, then you made your own mind up personally at the end, and then it ends 'then I hope you've decided what *you* think' — the reader is asked to decide for himself, or herself.

S: Well really you've got to decide for yourself. There is no-one who can say that one thing is right and one thing is wrong, its a matter of your own decision.

VIDEOTAPE RECORDER

The videotape recorder is increasingly being used by teachers as a means of gathering general information about their teaching. It allows the teacher to observe many facets of his or her teaching quickly, and provides heuristic and accurate information for diagnosis. After this, the teacher may wish to use a different method to examine specific aspects of his or her teaching.

Many of the teacher-researchers I know use the video on an intermittent but regular basis to enable them to keep in touch with their teaching. If an observer or student can be used to operate the video-recorder, then more attention can be paid to specific teaching episodes (identified beforehand) or the reaction of particular students.

Two concerns related to the videotape recorder are cost and its disruptive influence (because of its novelty) on classroom behaviour patterns. Increasingly, many schools have a video-recorder at their disposal, and because few teachers actually research their teaching, video-machines are often available. Secondly, the novelty value of the equipment rapidly disappears with use. I advise teachers to introduce the equipment to the pupils first, demonstrate how it works and then leave it standing in the classroom for some time before actually taping. This allows both the pupils and teachers to become accustomed to its presence. Another tip is to keep the monitor switched off except during demonstration sessions.

The main advantages and disadvantages of the videotape recorder are listed in point form in Box 8.5. Three uses of video-recorders in classroom research are:

- for obtaining visual material of the total teaching situation
- acting as an aid to diagnosis, and
- as a means of examining in detail a specific teaching episode.

Box 8.5

ADVANTAGES	DISADVANTAGES
• Enables all situations to be constantly reviewed • Origin of problems can be diagnosed • Behavioural patterns of teacher and pupil can be seen • Patterns of progress over long periods can be clearly charted	• Expensive to obtain • Can be very conspicuous and distracting • If camera is directed by operator, it will only record that which he or she deems to be of importance; operator acts as editor

In this example I describe the first experience Geoff, a student on one of my in-service courses, had with the videotape recorder.

Geoff is a deputy head teacher in a special school. His pupils are severely impaired, but the expectation is that they will eventually be able to cope by themselves in some limited way. To give his pupils that basic level of life-skill is Geoff's main goal. Geoff used the video to examine his teaching and to try and find an answer to the question 'why is everything so time-consuming?'.

Geoff decided to video the morning session from 9:30 to 10:15, which was the most structured and high energy time of the day. During the lesson, the nursery nurse was also involved in the class. Before videoing, Geoff identified a series of topics that he wanted to get information on:

- maximum time worked by each pupil,
- time wasted by each pupil,
- time unavoidably lost,

- time to be spent with each pupil, and
- number of tasks accomplished in the 45-minute session by each pupil.

The videotaping session went well. Geoff had had the camera in his room for a few days, so the pupils were used to having it around. With a wide-angle lens he was able to capture all the activity in the class. Geoff then began reviewing the tape. Besides gathering data on the points above, he also detailed the following:

- amount of time he spent out of the class on administrative duties,
- the number of times he praised/reprimanded a pupil,
- how long the pupils were left unsupervised,
- time spent by nursery nurse with each pupil, and
- pupil's reaction to attention.

Geoff then analysed the tape for each pupil and produced a detailed analysis of how individual lessons were spent. From this information Geoff was able to derive a number of hypotheses concerning the class and set up a programme for utilizing the time more effectively.

QUESTIONNAIRES

Questionnaires that ask specific questions about aspects of the classroom, curriculum or teaching method are a quick and simple way of obtaining broad and rich information from pupils. It is important, however, particularly in the primary grades, to be relatively unsophisticated in the

Fig. 8.1

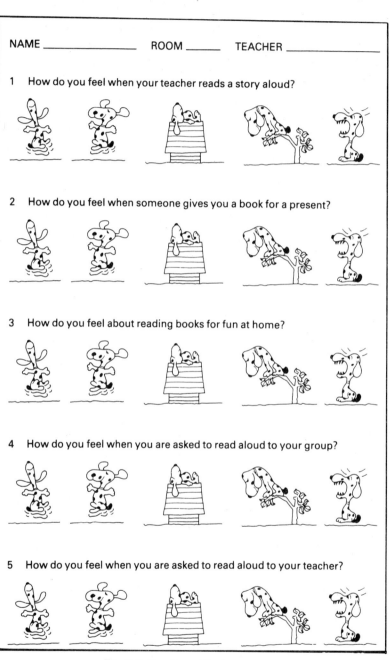

Fig. 8.2 Reading attitude survey.

structuring of the questions. Condense the usual 5-point scale to two or three responses, keep the questions simple, and use the basic 'what did you like best', 'what did you like least', 'what would you do differently' type of open-ended question.

With younger (and older) pupils it is often more profitable to use a happy face as the criterion response to questions as in Fig. 8.1 More imaginatively, cartoon pictures can be used, as in Fig. 8.2 – the possibilities are endless!

The main advantages and disadvantages of the questionnaire are listed in point form in Box 8.6. The main use of the questionnaire in classroom research is to obtain quantitative responses to specific predetermined questions. Examples of questionnaires are given in Figs 8.2 and 8.3.

Box 8.6

ADVANTAGES	DISADVANTAGES
• Easy to administer; quick to fill in • Easy to follow up • Provides direct comparison of groups and individuals • Provides feedback on: – attitudes – adequacy of resources – adequacy of teacher help – preparation for next session – conclusions at end of term • Data are quantifiable	• Analysis is time-consuming • Extensive preparation to get clear and relevant questions • Difficult to get questions that explore in depth • Effectiveness depends very much on reading ability and comprehension of the child • Children may be fearful of answering candidly • Children will try to produce 'right' answers

---

Inquiry/discovery follow-up questionnaire

Please put a ring round the answer you wish to give to each question. If you are not sure ring the nearest to what you think.

1	How much of the lesson did you enjoy?	All of it/Some of it/None
2	How much do you think you learnt?	Nothing/Something/A lot
3	How much did you understand?	Most of it/Some of it/Nothing
4	Could you find the books, information, equipment you needed?	None/Some of it/Most of it
5	Did other people help you?	A lot/A little/Not at all
6	Did other people stop you working?	A lot/Sometimes/Not at all
7	Did the teacher help you	Enough/Not enough
8	Did the lesson last	Long enough/Too long/Not long enough
9	Was the lesson	Boring/Interesting
10	Did you need anything you could not find?	Yes/No
11	Where did you get help from?	Teacher/Group/Someone else
12	Did you find this work	Easy/Hard/Just about right
13	Write down anything which made it hard for you to learn	
14	Write down anything you particularly enjoyed about this lesson	

Fig. 8.3 A sample questionnaire designed by Roger Pols. Reproduced with permission from Bowen *et al.* (n.d.).

SOCIOMETRY

Sociometric analysis or sociometry is a technique used to measure the emotional structure of a group. As a diagnostic instrument, sociometry's purpose is to highlight the feelings of attraction, indifference and rejection that occur within a group and between its members. The approach has obvious applications to classrooms where teachers want to discover the social structure of the class for research and other purposes. The most important 'other purpose' is to identify pupils who are socially isolated in order to take remedial action.

Before administering a sociometric test, it is important to ensure that the pupils know each other fairly well, that confidentiality is established, and that action be taken as a consequence. Sociometry in this sense is a dynamic process that can lead to improvement in children's attitudes and relationships and the general enhancement of a classroom climate.

Congdon (1978: 6) describes a method for administering the sociometric test:

> Each child is handed a slip of blank paper and told to write his name at the top. Some teachers prefer to have the names of all pupils in the class written on the blackboard. It is always advisable to write up the names of any pupils who are absent. The test should be meaningful to the pupils. So, for example, the context of the test could be a project. After deciding on a project the pupils could be told that they will be allowed to work in groups and that the groups would be made up according to their own choices.
>
> On the left hand side of the sheet the pupils are asked to write the name of the person with whom they would most like to work in a group. Underneath they are asked to write the name of the one they would like next best, then the next and so on. They can be told to write as many names as they wish or none at all. The pupil is then asked to turn over the sheet and again down the left hand side of the page to write the names of any children with whom they do not wish to work. The teacher again tells them that they may write as many names as they wish or none at all. And what is more important she tells them that the names will be known only to herself, i.e. the choices are made privately and no pupil should be told either who chose him or how many choices he received. In this way no one's feelings are hurt.

After the test has been administered, the pupil choices are analysed to establish the structure of relationships within the class. The best known and easiest understood method of doing this is the sociogram. Congdon (1978: 7) continues to describe how a sociogram is constructed:

> In drawing a sociogram it is often useful to begin with the most chosen pupil and add the symbols for any pupils who reciprocate his or her choices. Next, pupils who have mutual choices with this group can be added. When these have been exhausted then a fresh group can be drawn up starting with the next most highly-chosen pupil and so on. The sociogram can be completed by filling in the unreciprocated choices.

Figure 8.4 is an example of a sociogram for a group of eight individuals with the symbols most commonly used marked on it.

Clearly, in Fig. 8.4 pupils E, F and H are unpopular and this information encourages the teacher to act to remedy this situation; action that can also be monitored through other classroom research techniques. The sociogram is a useful method for teacher-researchers who wish to explore the social structure of their class and the relationships between pupils. It also provides a starting point for action and further research. As sociometry emphasizes the class as a group, parallel efforts could focus on the perspectives of individual children, using, for example, self-concept inventories.

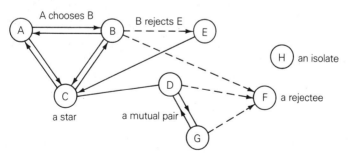

Fig. 8.4 Example of a sociogram.

Box 8.7

ADVANTAGES	DISADVANTAGES
• Simple way to discover social relationships in class • Provides guide to action • Can be integrated into class activity	• Possibility of compounding the isolation of some pupils

The major advantages and disadvantages of sociometry are listed in point form in Box 8.7. The main use of sociometry in classroom research is to disclose the social structure of the class.

In this example Ann was using a behaviour modification 'game' to improve the level of assignment completion in her maths class.

Since I had scruples about such a game causing social rejection of the target pupils, a sociogram was done before and after the experiment. Pupils were each asked to name three children they would like to sit next to during art lessons or storytime. It was stressed that this would be a non-academic, non-competitive time. The first choices were assigned three points, the second two points and the third one point. Points were totalled and the results entered on a graph.

Pre- and post-use of the sociogram showed that the popularity of the target pupils was not detrimentally affected by the game. None of them were social isolates but they all fell into the lower half of the class.

DOCUMENTARY EVIDENCE

Documents (memos, letters, position papers, examination papers, newspaper clippings, etc.) surrounding a curriculum

Box 8.8

ADVANTAGES	DISADVANTAGES
• Illuminate issues surrounding a curriculum or teaching method • Provide context, background and understanding • Provide an easy way of obtaining other people's perceptions	• Obtaining documents can be time-consuming • Certain documents may be difficult to obtain • Certain persons may be unwilling to share 'confidential' documents

or other educational concern can illuminate rationale and purpose in interesting ways. The use of such material can provide background information and understanding of issues that would not otherwise be available.

The main advantages and disadvantages of documentary evidence are listed in point form in Box 8.8. The main use of documents in classroom research is that they provide a context for understanding a particular curriculum or teaching method.

In this example Gill used documents to understand the nature of the art curriculum.

During her work for a postgraduate degree, Gill, an art teacher, examined some of the influences on the art curriculum. Her reason for doing this was largely personal: increasingly she was feeling a tension between her aspirations for art teaching and the general approach to the art curriculum that she was being encouraged to adopt. Gill's approach to the teaching of art was essentially child-centred. She has a commitment to developing a pupil's artistic talents and her teaching style and the activities she set her pupils were designed to achieve this goal. Her investigation involved examining a range of past papers and examiners' comments. To her chagrin, she found that the art curriculum in general was influenced not by pupil achievement or aspirations but more by the examiners' (rather traditional) comments. This discovery served at least to explain her tension. It also encouraged her to develop a scheme of work in painting for younger pupils and propose alternative syllabi for examination pupils that integrated her own ideas on art teaching with the more traditional approach.

SLIDE/TAPE AND VIDEO STILL PHOTOGRAPHY

Photographs and slides, with or without audiotape commentary, and the more recent use of a video stills camera, are useful ways of recording critical incidents in classrooms or of illustrating particular teaching episodes. They can also be used to support other forms of data gathering (e.g. interviews or field notes) or as a means for providing reference points for interviews or discussions.

The main advantages and disadvantages of slide/tape and video stills photography are listed in point form in Box 8.9. The full use of a video stills camera in classroom research as a means of illustrating critical incidents, and of provoking

Box 8.9

ADVANTAGES	DISADVANTAGES
• Advantage may be obtained by looking at images of kids working, or at end products of their work, and as a stimulus for discussion	• Shows isolated situations; difficulty of being in the right place at the right time; concentrates on small groups and individuals, not classes; records nothing in depth
• As an instrument which helps you get observation and comment from other teachers who were not present at the time	• Images may not truly depict activities of the children, if photographer is selective

discussion, is still to be explored. Rob Walker and Clem Adelman's (1975) *A Guide to Classroom Observation* contains advice on, and examples of, the use of photography in classroom research.

CASE STUDY

The case study is a relatively formal analysis of an aspect of classroom life. One way of producing a teacher research case study is described in the first section of Chapter 10. Some teachers may wish to produce case studies for a university course they are taking or as research towards a higher degree. These situations apart, it is unlikely that teachers will devote time to producing a formal case report of their teacher-researcher efforts every time they undertake a project.

The main advantages and disadvantages of the case study are listed in point form in Box 8.10. The main use of the case study in classroom research is that it provides a relatively

Box 8.10

ADVANTAGES	DISADVANTAGES
• A relatively simple way of plotting the progress of a course or a pupil's or group's reaction to teaching methods	• In order for the case study to be of value it must be fairly exhaustive; this means that it will be time-consuming in its preparation and its writing
• Information yielded by case studies will tend to give a more accurate and representative picture than will any one of the research methods detailed above; case studies draw on data gathered by many methods	• Feedback available to teacher only after considerable lapse of time

formal and fairly definitive analysis of a specific aspect of teaching behaviour or classroom life. Examples of teacher research case studies are given in Chapters 2 and 6.

In this chapter, I have described a variety of ways in which data can be gathered for the purpose of classroom research. The techniques described in this chapter are basically open-ended in so far as they are used most effectively for diagnostic purposes. Although I have described these techniques individually, it is important to realize that they can and are most often used eclectically and in combination. But each has a specific purpose and is best suited to a particular situation. A taxonomy of the main advantages, disadvantages and uses of the various techniques is given in Table 8.1.

FURTHER READING

Additional information about the techniques of classroom research can be found in the publications associated with the Ford Teaching Project. Elliott and Adelman's (1976) case study of the Ford Teaching Project in the Open University curriculum course *Innovation at the Classroom Level* is informative and useful, as is the Ford Teaching Project booklet *Ways of Doing Research in One's Own Classroom* (Bowen *et al.*, n.d.). Walker and Adelman's (1975) book *A Guide to Classroom Observation* is similarly helpful. Rob Walker's (1985) more recent book *Doing Research* contains detailed advice about methods, as does James McKernan's (1991) *Curriculum Action Research*. Colin Hook's (1981) *Studying Classrooms* is extensive and practical and also contains a useful taxonomy of approaches similar to Table 8.1. Kemmis and McTaggart's (1988) third edition of *The Action Research Planner* and John Elliott's (1991) *Action Research for Educational Change* also contain helpful advice.

Table 8.1 Taxonomy of classroom research techniques

Technique	Advantage(s)	Disadvantage(s)	Use(s)
Field notes	simple; ongoing; personal; aide-mémoire	subjective; needs practice	• specific issue • case study • general impression
Audiotape recording	versatile; accurate; provides ample data	transcription difficult; time-consuming; often inhibiting	• detailed evidence • diagnostic
Pupil diaries	provides pupils' perspective	subjective	• diagnostic • triangulation
Interviews and discussions	can be teacher–pupil, observer–pupil, pupil–pupil	time-consuming	• specific in-depth information
Videotape recorder	visual and comprehensive	awkward and expensive; can be distracting	• visual material • diagnostic
Questionnaires	highly specific; easy to administer; comparative	time-consuming to analyse; problem of 'right' answers	• specific information and feedback
Sociometry	easy to administer; provides guide to action	can threaten isolated pupils	• analyses social relationships
Documentary evidence	illuminative	difficult to obtain; time-consuming	• provides context and information
Slide/tape, video stills photography	illuminative; promotes discussion	difficult to obtain; expensive	• illustrates critical incidents
Case study	accurate; representative; uses range of techniques	time-consuming	• comprehensive overview of an issue • publishable format

CHAPTER 9

Analysing Classroom Research Data

The third criterion for teacher research outlined in Chapter 4 was that the methodology employed must be reliable enough to allow teachers confidently to formulate hypotheses and develop strategies applicable to their classroom situations. This is an area where teacher research in particular, and qualitative research in general, has not been conspicuously successful. Qualitative research procedures (i.e. where the emphasis is on expressing one's data and conclusions in the form of words) seem often to be shrouded in mystery. The findings of such studies are arrived at by usually unannounced procedures and techniques, thus creating methodologies which can be neither fully scrutinized nor usefully emulated. Consequently, it is important to establish a coherent methodology for analysing classroom research data. In this chapter, I first outline the problem in a little more detail, then suggest a framework for analysis and describe the four stages that comprise the process.

THE PROBLEM

Action research, like most practitioner-oriented method-ologies, has been widely criticized, but mainly by those who implicitly denigrate the method by criticizing individual research projects that have adopted classroom research techniques. It is illogical – not to say unfair – to judge the quality of a Shakespeare play by observing a performance by amateur actors. And so it is with classroom research.

It is true though that classroom research is often done badly, often because of unarticulated procedures for analysis. By way of contrast, the rules for quasi-experimental research have been cogently articulated (Campbell and Stanley 1963) and have a long and distinguished tradition. This tradition is so prevalent that research in education is commonly equated with studies carried out under this paradigm. This should not be surprising, for the rules are simple to apply and are consistent with the ubiquitous psycho-statistical research tradition. It is unfortunate, as we have seen, that this approach is ill-suited to the research needs of the classroom teacher.

In classroom research, the concern is more with cases than samples. This implies a methodology more applicable to understanding a problematic situation than one based on predicting outcomes within the parameters of an existing and tacitly accepted social system. The skills required of classroom researchers are, as Strauss and Corbin (1990: 18) note, 'The ability to step back and critically analyze situations, to recognize and avoid bias, to obtain valid and reliable data, and to think abstractly.'

Unfortunately, as Miles and Huberman (1984a: 20) note in their paper 'Drawing valid meaning from qualitative data', there is an Achilles heel here: there are few agreed canons for the analysis of qualitative data, and therefore the truth claims and validity underlying such work are uncertain. They describe the problem like this:

> Despite a growing interest in qualitative studies, we lack a body of clearly defined methods for drawing

valid meaning from qualitative data. We need methods that are practical, communicable, and not self deluding: scientific in the positivist's sense of the word, and aimed toward interpretive understanding in the best sense of that term.

What follows is an attempt to rectify this situation, at least with regards to teacher-based classroom research.

A FRAMEWORK FOR ANALYSIS

Making sense of social situations has long been the task of sociologists and it is from their (and anthropologists') methodological canons that much recent avant-garde work on educational evaluation has been drawn (see Hamilton *et al.* 1977). It is this research tradition that provides a framework within which to consider teacher-based classroom research. Classrooms are also complex social situations that require understanding. We need to produce theory that is applicable to classrooms as well as within them.

Two of the classic statements on sociological fieldwork were made by Becker (1958) and Glaser and Strauss (1967). In his paper 'Problems of inference and proof in participant observation', Becker (1958: 653) describes four stages in the analysis of fieldwork data:

> We can distinguish three distinct stages of analysis conducted in the field itself, and a fourth stage, carried on after completion of the field work. These stages are differentiated, first, by their logical sequence: each succeeding stage depends on some analysis in the preceding stage. They are further differentiated by the fact that different kinds of conclusions are arrived at in each stage and that these conclusions are put to different uses in the continuing research. Finally, they

are differentiated by the different criteria that are used to assess evidence and to reach conclusions in each stage. The three stages of field analysis are: the selection and definition of problems, concepts, and indices; the check on the frequency and distribution of phenomena; and the incorporation of individual findings into a model of the organisation under study. The fourth stage of final analysis involves problems of presentation of evidence and proof.

In a similar way, in *The Discovery of Grounded Theory*, Glaser and Strauss (1967: 105) describe the concept of the constant comparative method as a means of analysing sociological data:

> We shall describe in four stages the constant comparative method; 1. comparing incidents applicable to each category, 2. integrating categories and their properties, 3. delimiting the theory, and 4. writing the theory. Although this method of generating theory is a continuously growing process – each stage after a time is transformed into the next – earlier stages do remain in operation simultaneously throughout the analysis and each provides continuous development to its successive stage until the analysis is terminated.

Although Glaser and Strauss' notion of the constant comparative method is a more dynamic concept than Becker's linear sequence of stages, there are basic similarities in their approaches to the analysis of field data. Each envisage the analytical process as having four distinct generic stages: (1) data collection and the initial generation of categories, (2) validation of categories, (3) interpretation of categories and (4) action. These various stages are summarized in Table 9.1 and represent standard practice for the analysis of qualitative field data. My major point is that this same process can be used by teachers to analyse data emerging from their own classroom research efforts.

Table 9.1 Fieldwork methodology

Classroom research	Becker	Glaser and Strauss
• Data collection	• Selection and definition of concepts	• Compare incidents applicable to each category
• Validation	• Frequency and distribution of concepts	• Integrate categories and their phenomena
• Interpretation	• Incorporation of findings into model	• Delimit theory
• Action	• Presentation of evidence and proof	• Write theory

JANE: AN EXAMPLE

As part of the requirements for a course I taught on the 'Analysis of Teaching', Jane made a videotape of herself experimenting with various models of teaching. After reviewing the videotape, Jane felt that among other observations she had been rather abrupt in her questioning technique and had given the pupils little time to formulate responses to her questions. I suggested to Jane that she explore this observation a little further and ascertain whether this was a consistent behaviour or an aberration. She did this by taking a further videotape of her teaching, and by asking a colleague to observe her teaching. Jane also developed a short questionnaire on her questioning technique, which she administered to her pupils and subsequently analysed. As a result of this endeavour, Jane realized that she did in fact interject very quickly after asking a question, and quite often answered her own questions. All well and good, Jane thought, but what does this mean? Thinking that recent research on teaching might help, Jane did some reading and came across an article on think-time. The article reviewed a number of studies on the relationship between the amount of time that elapsed after questioning and the quality of pupil response. Jane felt that she was not allowing her pupils enough time to think after she had asked a question to the detriment perhaps of their level of cognitive functioning. So she developed a plan to change and monitor her questioning technique. It took Jane some six months to complete these tasks (teaching is a time-consuming job!), but there was no pressure on her to complete the research. In fact, the longer time-frame allowed for more valid data, and she was pleased with the results. Not only did she find evidence of higher-level responses from her pupils, but also, by involving them in the evaluation of her teaching, the climate of her class was enhanced by the mutual and overt commitment of both teacher and pupils to the learning process.

DATA COLLECTION

In the classroom research process, the first step is collecting data. With the use of, say, a videotape recorder, or any other of a range of methods, the teacher gathers information about his or her teaching. Having collected the data, a substage follows immediately or co-exists with the collection of data – the generation of hypotheses. We are always generating ideas to explain classroom events. Even at the earliest stages of research, we are interpreting and explaining to ourselves 'why this is happening' and 'what caused that'. It is inevitable that as individuals we bring our experience and beliefs to bear upon situations that we wish to understand better. As Popper says, 'observations . . . are always interpretations of the facts observed . . . they are interpretations in the light of theories' (quoted in Magee 1973: 107). Popper's use of the word theory implies, of course, not only 'grand' theory, but also personal theory – the presuppositions, assumptions and beliefs that guide our actions.

At the end of the data collection stage, not only have we collected our data, but we have also established a number of hypotheses, constructs or categories that begin to explain what is happening in the classroom. These hypotheses (I am using the word eclectically) usually emerge quite naturally from the data-gathering process. Jane, in the example, generated a number of ideas about her teaching from viewing the videotape. Among these was an observation that she was too abrupt in her questioning technique and had given her pupils too little time to answer questions. These hypotheses not only reflect the data but are also an interpretation of them. At this stage, the more ideas the better. The richer and more creative our thoughts, the more likely it is that the research will result in a coherent and complete interpretation of the problem. It is in the following stage that we begin to evaluate the hypotheses, so initially one should be as creative and as suggestive as possible.

VALIDATION

The second stage in the process concerns the validation of the hypotheses. I will suggest a number of techniques for establishing the validity of a category or hypothesis. Of all these 'tests for trustworthiness', triangulation is most probably the best known, and so I describe it first.

The technique of *triangulation* was popularized by John Elliott and Clem Adelman during their work with the Ford Teaching Project. It involves contrasting the perceptions of one actor in a specific situation against those of other actors in the same situation. By doing this, an initial subjective observation or perception is fleshed out and given a degree of authenticity. Elliott and Adelman (1976: 74) describe the technique thus:

> Triangulation involves gathering accounts of a teaching situation from three quite different points of view; namely those of the teacher, his pupils, and a partici-

pant observer. Who in the 'triangle' gathers the accounts, how they are elicited, and who compares them, depends largely on the context. The process of gathering accounts from three distinct standpoints has an epistemological justification. Each point of the triangle stands in a unique epistemological position with respect to access to relevant data about a teaching situation. The teacher is in the best position to gain access via introspection to his own intentions and aims in the situation. The students are in the best position to explain how the teacher's actions influence the way they respond in the situation. The participant observer is in the best position to collect data about the observable features of the interaction between teachers and pupils. By comparing his own account with accounts from the other two standpoints a person at one point of the triangle has an opportunity to test and perhaps revise it on the basis of more sufficient data.

Jane, in the example, validated her observations through triangulation. She had another teacher observe her teaching and she also gave her pupils a questionnaire on her questioning technique. From this evidence, she was able to validate and refine the observation from three different sources.

It must be admitted that triangulation is not always an easy process to engage in. Initially, it may be threatening for a teacher to involve students in the evaluation of their teaching, or it may prove difficult to obtain the services of a peer to act as a participant observer. Teachers with the personal openness and interest in their teaching needed to initiate such research will, however, eventually overcome these difficulties. Incidentally, I believe that it is important for the teacher to involve his or her pupils in the research process as soon as their confidence allows. Children provide wonderfully frank and honest feedback, especially when they sense that their opinions are valued and respected, and this can only serve to enhance the quality of life in the classroom. The teacher must, however, be careful to introduce this change in his or her teaching slowly and self-consciously, being fully aware that pupils are a potentially conservative force within the classroom and often need to be 'broken in' to new ideas and different styles (Rudduck 1984).

Another well-known technique is *saturation*. Becker (1958) and Glaser and Strauss (1967) point to a similar process: Becker refers to 'the check on the frequency and distribution of phenomenon' (p. 653) and Glaser and Strauss to 'saturation', a situation where 'no additional data are being found . . . [to] develop properties of the category' (p. 67). When applied to the classroom research situation, this implies that the hypothesis or category generated from observation is tested repeatedly against the data in an attempt to modify or falsify it.

It is difficult and perhaps reckless to suggest a frequency that ensures the validity of a category, for that will vary from case to case, but during this process a number of predictable events can occur. First, if on repeated testing the category is found wanting it is then discarded. Second, the category may have been conceptualized crudely and, through testing, the concept is modified, refined and amplified. Third, although the process of falsification (in the Popperian sense) is never complete, there comes a time when repeated observation leads neither to refutation nor amplification and only serves to support the hypothesis. At this point, when the utility of observation decreases, saturation can be said to have occurred and the hypothesis has been validated.

Referring to the example of Jane, having decided to explore her questioning technique further, she videotaped herself again and found that, in fact, she was quite abrupt in her questioning and interjected far too quickly. In this way, she firmly validated the observation by saturating it.

There are a number of other techniques for establishing validity which I will describe more briefly. But before I do, I should distinguish between *validity*, which reflects the internal consistency of one's research, and *reliability*, which reflects the generalizability of one's findings. In general, most classroom researchers and those who use qualitative methods are concerned with validity rather than reliability; in so far as their focus is a particular case rather than a sample.

In the same way as one triangulates the perception of various individuals, so too must we triangulate our *sources of data*. There are, as we have seen, many data sources open to the classroom researcher, e.g. surveys, questionnaires, observation, interviews and documents. The matrix shown later in Fig. 9.1 helps illustrate the range of data sources available at different levels of analysis. Although not every cell should be completed, a wide scatter should usually be employed. Each data source gives information of a different type which usually serves to complement and provide a check on the others.

Two other common techniques used at this stage of analysis are *rival explanations* and the search for *negative cases*. Michael Patton (1980: 327–8) describes these techniques like this:

> When considering rival hypotheses and competing explanations the strategy to be employed is not one of attempting to disprove the alternatives; rather, the analyst looks for data that *support* alternative explanations. Failure to find strong supporting evidence for alternative explanations helps increase confidence in the original, principal explanation.
>
> Closely related to the testing of alternative explanations is the search for negative cases. Where patterns and trends have been identified, our understanding of those patterns and trends is increased by considering the instances and cases that do not fit within the pattern.

I use the phrase *call things by their right name* to describe the next technique, which is nicely illustrated by Humpty Dumpty when he said: 'When I use a word it means just what I choose it to mean – neither more or less.' The point is an obvious one – we need to know what we are looking for. As classroom researchers, we have to do our conceptual work properly. We should be aware, for example, of suggesting that a child who is looking intently at a teacher is in fact paying attention; or of dictionary definitions that define intelligence as mental ability; or of operational definitions that regard paying attention as not looking out of the window. None of these help us very much. Conceptualization involves articulating a full, clear and coherent account of what constitutes being an instance of something; that is to say, it necessitates elaborating the criteria that have to be met if, for example, a pupil is legitimately to be described as engaging in enquiry/discovery learning (Barrow 1986). This may be difficult to do at the outset, but the clarification of concepts should always be a major concern throughout the research process.

An *audit trail* is a fairly recent technique used to increase the validity of one's data and which borrows its name from the concept of a financial audit. Schwandt and Halpern (1988: 73) describe the usefulness of an audit trail, or of establishing a chain of evidence, in this way:

> Preparing an audit trail is important for two reasons. First, it documents the inquiry in a fashion that facilitates a third-party examination. The audit trail contains information that describes the methods used to control error and to reach justifiable conclusions. . . Second, an audit trail helps [classroom researchers] manage their record keeping. They find an organized trail useful when they need to retrieve information easily and when they prepare their final reports . . . [it helps them] become more thoughtful, critical, and reflective.

Another widely used strategy for ensuring validity is having *key respondents* review drafts of one's research reports. This can either be the people involved in the research (one's colleagues or students), or those knowledgeable about the situation you are enquiring into. To the extent that those involved in the research do not recognize the description and analysis in the report, then its validity is suspect. Involving others in the research is also a worthwhile activity in itself.

Let me now restate the important methodological point. I am arguing that by employing analytical techniques such as triangulation and the other methods just described, teacher-researchers can produce hypotheses and concepts that are valid, methodologically sound and to an extent generalizable.

By engaging in this process of hypothesis generation, teacher-researchers are producing what Glaser and Strauss have called grounded theory, because it is theory grounded in data gathered from and applicable to a specific social situation. By utilizing this methodology, we can have confidence in our subsequent actions for, as Dunn and Swierczek (1977: 137) comment:

> The application of grounded theories promises to contribute to improvements in the degree to which findings 1. reflect conditions actually present in particular change efforts (internal validity); 2. typify conditions actually present in other change efforts (external validity); 3. contribute to the generation of new concepts by constantly comparing information obtained by different methods (reflexivity); and 4. promote understanding among groups with conflicting frames of reference.

INTERPRETATION

The third stage in the research process is interpretation. This involves taking a validated hypothesis and fitting it into a frame of reference that gives it meaning. For the classroom researcher, this means taking a hypothesis and relating it either to theory, the norms of accepted practice or the teacher's own intuition as to what comprises good teaching. This allows the teacher-researcher to give meaning to a particular observation or series of observations that can lead profitably to action. In doing this, the classroom researcher is creating meaning out of hitherto discrete observations and constructs.

Jane gave meaning to her hypothesis by reading about 'think-time'. That information not only helped her understand the implications of her behaviour but also suggested a direction for action.

ACTION

The final step in the process is action. Having created meaning out of the research data, the teacher-researcher is in a position to plan for future action. Building on the evidence gathered during the research, the teacher is able to plan realistic strategies which are themselves monitored by classroom research procedures. Jane did just that. The interpretation stage gave her information on how to change her questioning technique, which after some planning she attempted to monitor and evaluate.

THE ONGOING PROCESS OF DATA ANALYSIS

The analysis of data is a very important part of the classroom research process. It is only at this stage that the teacher can be certain that the results obtained are valid and trustworthy. When teacher-researchers fail to analyse their data adequately, they lack a secure platform for action. The four stages of classroom research are outlined in Box 9.1.

The four stages of classroom research, although based on sociological research methods, are, in fact, only organized common sense. These stages are also far more interactive than the linear description given so far in this chapter

Box 9.1

Four Stages of Classroom Research

1 *Data collection* and the generation or categories of hypotheses.

2 *Validation* of categories or hypotheses using the techniques for trustworthiness, such as triangulation.

3 *Interpretation* by reference to theory, agreed criteria, established practice or teacher judgement.

4 *Action* for development that is also monitored by classroom research techniques.

would imply. In fact, the whole process is in reality a very dynamic one. There are two aspects of this 'dynamism' that I want to mention in particular.

In Fig. 9.1, there is a matrix that illustrates the range of data sources available at each stage of analysis. As noted earlier, not every cell of the matrix needs to be completed! The point to be made here is that in the initial phase, one analyses the questionnaire or interview schedules. Then uses the analysed data from a number of different sources to generate the categories or hypotheses. Having done that, one validates them in the second phase and then returns to phase one to collect more data. This ongoing process of data collection and verification is a characteristic of the analysis of qualitative or naturalistic research data.

The second point is that the *whole* process is interactive. Matthew Miles and Michael Huberman, whose concern about the lack of agreement on methods for analysis we have already noted, have written a very practical and detailed book called *Qualitative Data Analysis*. In it they describe the interactive model of data analysis like this (Miles and Huberman 1984b: 21–2):

> *Data Reduction*: Data reduction refers to the process of selecting, focusing, simplifying, abstracting and transforming the 'raw' data that appear in written up field notes. As data collection proceeds, there are further episodes of data reduction (doing summaries,

Analysis

	Information source				
	Surveys	_Questionnaires_	_Observations_	_Interviews_	_Documents_
1 Data collection and the generation of categories or hypotheses					
2 Validation of categories or hypotheses					
3 Interpretation by reference to theory, agreed criteria, established practice or teacher judgement					
4 Plan action for development					

Fig. 9.1 A matrix for analysing classroom research data.

coding, teasing out themes, making clusters, making partitions, writing memos). And the data reduction/ transforming process continues after fieldwork, until a final report is complete.

Data Display: The second major flow of analysis activity is data display. We define a 'display' as an organised assembly of information that permits conclusion drawing and action taking. Looking at displays helps us to understand what is happening and to do something – further analysis or action – based on that understanding.

Conclusion Drawing/Verification: The third stream of analysis activity is conclusion drawing and verification. From the beginning of data collection, the [classroom researcher] is beginning to decide what things mean, is noting regularities, patterns, explanations, possible configurations, causal flows and propositions. The competent researcher holds these conclusions lightly, maintaining openness and scepticism, but the conclusions are still there, inchoate and vague at first, then increasingly explicit and grounded.

In this sense, qualitative data analysis is a continuous, iterative enterprise. Issues of data reduction of display, and of conclusion drawing/verification come into figure successfully as analysis episodes follow each other.

The dynamics of the analysis stage adds to the complexity of what is already the most difficult part of the classroom research process. The procedures described in this chapter, however, make good working guidelines in any form of qualitative enquiry, be it to inform the thought processes of a group of teachers sitting together for an hour to discuss their classroom research, or researchers involved in an international multi-site case study. Qualitative research is less of a methodology and more a way of life! It is an approach that is applicable across a range of settings, describes and analyses phenomena on their own terms, and helps us to think constructively and to generate meaning out of complex and problematic situations. Consequently, it is also an approach that empowers individuals and increases feelings of efficacy. This sense of efficacy can only develop if we share our methodological procedures and establish a genuinely collaborative and critical research community that is committed to informed action.

FURTHER READING

This is complex territory which I have tried to present as simply as I can in this chapter. More detailed accounts can be found in my *Evaluation for School Development* (Hopkins 1989: Ch. 5) and a recent paper (Hopkins *et al.* 1989). Since the mid-1970s, there has been a growing interest in illuminative, anthropological and ethnographic research approaches. Much of this literature is technical and not ideally suited for our purposes. However, a recent book by Hammersley and Atkinson (1983), *Ethnography: Principles in Practice*, provides an excellent overview of the field and an introduction to the literature. Lincoln and Guba's (1985) *Naturalistic Enquiry* is also a useful source, as is Patton's (1980) *Qualitative Evaluation Methods*. *Beyond the Numbers Game* (Hamilton *et al.* 1977) is a comprehensive statement on the illuminative or new wave tradition in educational evaluation and research, mainly from the UK perspective. One of the most helpful sections in this collection is the discussion of alternative methodology, especially the work of Louis Smith. Clem Adelman's book, *Uttering, Muttering* (1981), on linguistic research in classrooms contains an helpful chapter on triangulation. McCormick and James' (1988) book on *Curriculum Evaluation in Schools*, besides being an excellent general source, contains some very helpful sections on validity and reliability.

The references mentioned in the text should also be consulted, especially Becker (1958) and Glaser and Strauss (1967), although the latter may prove to be a little hard going. Fortunately, two recent books by Strauss (1987) and Strauss and Corbin (1990) prove more accessible. The first chapter of Strauss' *Qualitative Analysis for Social Scientists* provides an exemplary introduction to grounded theory. Anyone seriously interested in educational research should also be familiar with Campbell and Stanley's (1963) classic 'Experimental and quasi-experimental designs for research on teaching'. Although written from a different perspective from this book, its discussion of research designs and the concepts of internal and external validity are essential knowledge for those involved in educational research. Finally, Miles and Huberman's (1984b) *Qualitative Data Analysis* is *the* essential source book for anyone interested in the ideas and themes touched on in this chapter.

CHAPTER 10

Maintaining the Action

The link between research and action has been an implicit theme throughout this book. To teacher-researchers, research alone is a necessary but not sufficient condition: research has to feed action and development. The classroom research process described in previous chapters has as its goal professional development and the enhancement of classroom performance. The fourth stage in the analytical framework discussed in the last chapter was action, which itself is monitored and researched using classroom research procedures. This is the crowning achievement of the research process. In this chapter, I want to look at some of the ways in which the action, generated by the research process, can be maintained. I will discuss how teacher-researchers go about reporting their research, some issues involved in publication, the nature of collaborative action, curriculum, teaching and staff development.

REPORTING THE RESEARCH

There are a number of different ways of reporting teacher research efforts. I have seen them range from loose anecdotal accounts to highly 'scientific' and formal research reports submitted for a higher degree. In many instances, teachers who engage in classroom research have no need to present their results to anyone except to themselves; particularly if the research is to be used solely to enhance their teaching. Despite this, I think that all teacher-researchers need to put their data together in such a way that:

1 The research could be replicated on another occasion.
2 The evidence used to generate hypotheses and consequent action is clearly documented.
3 Action taken as a result of the research is monitored.
4 The reader finds the research accessible and that it resonates with his or her own experience.

This process of setting a clear purpose, of using a methodology which provides valid results, and then using these as a basis for action, can be made relatively straightforward if the researcher keeps a loose-leaf log or diary as the research progresses. An ongoing research diary like this also provides an invaluable basis for reflection and is great fun to look at with the wisdom of hindsight. It provides an excellent record of how one's views and attitudes evolve over time.

If one does want or need to prepare a research report, there are many ways of doing this. To begin with, there is the rather traditional approach which uses as a guide, points similar to the following:

1 *Statement of intent*
   • clarify purpose,
   • rationale.
2 *Procedures and process*
   • research design,
   • techniques of data collection,
   • verification of concepts,
   • what actually occurred.

3 *Results and implementation*
  - outcomes of research,
  - theoretical implications,
  - action taken as a result,
  - evaluation of action.
4 *Meta-analysis*
  - review whole process,
  - conclusions as to the usefulness of the research,
  - what would you do different next time.

The purpose of this approach is to provide teacher-researchers with a framework for their report. While this is important, what perhaps is even more critical is that the format of a report encourages the teacher to stand back and to examine the process systematically by making a meta-analysis of the research.

Classroom researchers should not feel constrained by the traditional research report format when sharing the product of their research. There are any number of formats that can be used. As long as the procedures outlined in previous chapters are followed, then imagination is the only limit on the possibilities of presentation. Here are a few examples:

1 *Cartoons*: often classroom researchers use the cartoon format to get a key finding from their research across in a powerful and accessible way.
2 *Video*: a visual representation using video or 'video stills' provides concrete images that an audience can relate to their own situation.
3 *Fiction*: using data or constructs from the research to tell a story often encourages reflection and discussion more effectively than the traditional report. As long as the quotations or events are 'real', then a fictional setting may enhance the message.
4 *Data reduction and display*: displaying reduced data is often a powerful way of stimulating discussion. This approach allows large amounts of data to be displayed

economically and it could be accompanied by another page of questions, commentary or explanation that highlighted the main issues.

Classroom researchers should not be afraid to experiment with different ways of presenting their work, as long as the information is valid and has been carefully analysed. The fundamental point is that action should result from the research.

Let us assume that some valid 'knowledge' has been generated by a classroom researcher. What key conditions must be present if someone is to take action congruent with the knowledge? Here, Louis and Miles (1990: 289) take a cut at what might be required:

Clarity:	The knowledge must be understood clearly – not be fuzzy, vague or confusing.
Relevance:	The knowledge is seen as meaningful, as connected to one's normal life and concerns – not irrelevant, inapplicable, impractical.
Action images:	The knowledge is or can become exemplified in specific actions, clearly visualized. Without such images, knowledge-based action is unlikely.
Will:	There must be motivation, interest, action orientation, a will to do something with the knowledge.
Skill:	There must be actual behavioural ability to do the action envisioned. Without skill, the action will either be aborted or done incongruently with the knowledge undergirding it.

Colin Hook (1981: 291–2), in his book *Studying Classrooms*, provides a helpful checklist of questions that can be used to review one's research report or any other format for presenting classroom research:

1 Did I collect the information as planned? Did it provide the information I needed?
2 What problems did I have? What could I have done better? Should I employ other data-gathering methods?
3 Did I gather all relevant available information? Should I have gathered pupils' opinions, parental views, other teachers' feelings?
4 In what ways can I use the information to make more effective teacher decisions? Is further information required?
5 Can the information obtained be interpreted in other ways? Are my interpretations and conclusions valid?
6 Have I presented the information in a clear way? Does the information indicate future teaching actions?
7 Can I discuss the information with pupils, colleagues or parents?
8 Who else could have been involved, how and when?
9 What did I, the pupils, parents, colleagues, etc., get out of the investigation?
10 What changes should I make in future investigations? Do my pupils, colleagues, etc., have suggestions?
11 Can I interest colleagues in co-ordinating action research approaches, to collaborate in future studies?
12 Do other teachers share my concerns? Do other teachers have skills which may help me in self-monitoring?

PUBLICATION AND RESEARCH

Mention of writing a research report raises the question of publication. As a precursor to the discussion, let me quote from Ebbutt (1985: 157):

> If action research is to be considered legitimately as research, the participants in it must, it seems to me, be prepared to produce written reports of their activities.

Moreover these reports ought to be available to some form of public critique. I would go as far as to say that if this condition is not satisfied by participants then no matter how personally and professionally valuable the exercise is in which they are engaged, it is not action research.

While I would agree with Ebbutt's call for written reports and critique, particularly by other teacher-researchers, I disagree with the implication that unless the research is published it is not research. It seems to me that many current commentators on classroom research have a misplaced conception of what research actually is.

An example of this is Jon Nixon's *A Teacher's Guide to Action Research* (1981). It is a collection of teacher research reports loosely gathered together, and varying in quality. Many of the essays are anecdotal and subjective, and provide no critical commentary on the process or behaviours they purport to describe. 'That's alright', its apologists claim, 'because it is not research, it is enquiry or self-monitoring'. And this is exactly the problem.

Michael Armstrong (1982) makes the distinction in a most beguiling way:

> I have grown impatient with the concept of 'research'. In the context of a study of education it has acquired too narrow a connotation especially in regard to criteria for rigour, evidence and validity. I prefer the word 'enquiry'. . . . The form of enquiry which I have in mind is grounded in the experience of teaching and in particular in that practice of sustained observation which is inseparable from good teaching. . .

Armstrong seems to be saying, 'Let's call it enquiry and let's keep it in the classroom and then we won't need to tangle with such questions as what counts as research.' Hull *et al.* (1985) complicate this position even further. They appear to say, 'let's call what Armstrong does self-monitoring (an investigation of one's own practice in private) but let's recognise that there is also teacher research'. They argue that teacher research:

> . . . must feed a tradition – from which individual researchers can derive support. In this way it is quite different from the activity which has been called 'self-monitoring' where a teacher uses some of the data-gathering techniques developed by researchers to record instances of their own practice as a basis for reflection. The self-monitoring teacher makes no claims to be methodologically reflexive. He or she does not undertake responsibility either to introduce 'system' into the investigations or make accounts of the studies available to other teachers. Self-monitoring is essentially a privatised encounter between a practitioner and practice. As such it has immense value. We conceive teacher research however, as potentially the root of a tradition of enquiry into educational processes which might stand alongside the academic tradition as an alternative body of knowledge rooted firmly in practice (Hull *et al.* 1983).

This statement is confused and problematic. The dichotomy that Armstrong and Hull and co-workers point to is just not there.

Armstrong's *Closely Observed Children* (1980) is one of the best teacher research studies. It is sensitive, insightful and profound; it is research at a high level of sophistication, imagination and rigour. Armstrong is doing teacher research in general, and himself in particular, a grave disservice to claim otherwise. One can readily appreciate Armstrong's 'impatience with the concept of research' – but to call it something else is not to change anything. He is impatient of narrowly defined psycho-statistical research that has little to say to teachers, not research *per se*.

Research, enquiry and self-monitoring are all aspects of a similar activity because they all require systematic, self-conscious and rigorous reflection to be of any value. The problem is that psychological research, with its emphasis on statistical manipulation, has captured the educational imagination to such an extent that most people cannot think of research in any other terms. But criteria, such as validity or internal consistency, are necessary if teacher-researchers are to escape the sentimental anecdote that often replaces statistical research designs in education, and gives teacher research such a bad name. Enquiry, self-monitoring and teacher research need to establish standards and criteria that are applicable to their area of activity, rather than assume (and then reject) criteria designed for different procedures.

Teacher research, like enquiry and self-monitoring, is a form of research. These forms may be presented to different audiences and formulated in different ways, but all are attempts to create meaning out of complex situations. And the meaning is only valid when it is subject to certain methodological standards. It is naive to argue that just because we call what we do enquiry or self-monitoring instead of research that we can escape the demand for valid judgement. That is throwing the baby out with the bath water. But, it is equally incorrect to assume that just because we engage in research, we have to follow the criteria of the psycho-statistical research paradigm. These criteria are inappropriate, and other more suitable methods, like the ones discussed in the previous chapter, have to be sought.

There are two important points to be drawn from this discussion. The first is that classroom research by teachers is a valid form of research because it results in hypotheses generated through a rigorous process of enquiry and grounded in the data to which they apply. This meets contemporary criteria for research. In the article to which I have already referred, Ebbutt (1985: 157) quotes:

> Shulman's conception of what counts as research; that it is 'a family of methods which share the characteristics of disciplined inquiry'. . .
>
> 1 arguments and evidence can be examined

2 not dependent solely on eloquence or surface plausibility

3 avoids sources of error when possible and discusses margin for possible errors in conclusion

4 can be speculative, free wheeling and inventive.

This, it seems to me, is an accurate description of research as it has been described in this book.

The second point is that it is important for teacher-researchers to open up their work to critique and, if possible, to publish it. The importance of public critique in classroom research is that it encourages a discourse among teachers which is research-oriented, and committed to action and the improvement of practice. It is the sharing of our experiences and the social and intellectual benefits that emanate from it, not the meeting of some abstract academic criteria, that provide the logic for publication and critique in classroom research. But the important point is that the mere fact of publication cannot be a judgement on the nature of the process that led (or did not lead) to publication.

In this section, I have argued strenuously against those who claim that teacher research is not really research. Their position is untenable because (1) it is a capitulation in the face of the norms of traditional research, (2) it devalues the quality of teacher research efforts and (3) it avoids the necessity of establishing a rigorous methodology for classroom research.

COLLABORATIVE ACTION

Despite the extensive preceding discussion, the *raison d'être* of classroom research is not publication but action. One of the most powerful forms of action is collaboration – sharing among teacher-researchers is critical. Each of the case studies reported in Chapter 2 involved or mentioned collaboration in classroom research. Indeed, the main purpose of the 'Developing Successful Learning Project' was partnership. Scattered throughout the examples in the book are illustrations of the ways in which teachers can support each other in classroom research efforts and the benefits all of those involved gain from it.

It is passé to talk about the 'sanctity of the classroom door' and the isolation that teachers work in. But, despite the various moves towards team teaching and collaboration, the classroom still remains in many cases an individual preserve. Yet, as we have seen, it is well established that teachers learn best from other teachers, so this vast potential for mutual improvement remains largely untapped. The involvement of another teacher in the research process greatly alleviates the sense of isolation and contributes towards increased purpose and commitment.

Here are three ways in which collaborative action for classroom research by teachers can be maintained: through attendance at in-service courses, the establishment of informal clubs and networks, and the inclusion of pupils in the research process.

Short in-service courses are still the dominant mode of professional development in the UK. Although the limitations of 'one shot' workshops for developing new skills and teaching strategies are well known, they still have some value (Rudduck 1981). Such courses provide an easy way to gain information about teacher research, they often provide a forum for the sharing of experience, and many courses provide some opportunities for practice and feedback. Perhaps, most importantly, they offer opportunities for networking and possibilities for future collaboration with other teachers. Many institutions of higher education, for example, offer courses on teacher research that deal with the knowledge and skills discussed in this book. The Classroom Action Research Network based at the Centre for Applied Research, University of East Anglia also sponsors courses and conferences on classroom research by teachers.

It is also not unknown for groups of teachers to form an *ad hoc* group (based perhaps on the local teachers' centre or

University) that acts as 'club' for teacher-researchers. Groups such as this, although not prolific, are an important potential resource for those teachers wishing to engage in classroom research and professional development activities. There are many other forms of networking, such as those based on schools that contain a number of teacher-researchers which expand to serve the teachers in the local area.

Another potential source of collaborative action is the pupils in one's own classroom. I have already mentioned the usefulness of pupil feedback for triangulation purposes, and the spin-off in terms of positive climate that occurs when pupils are involved in classroom research. I want to stress that point again here. It is entirely within the spirit of classroom research that pupils be involved in the process of improving the teaching–learning situation in their classrooms. The rewards for so doing, particularly in terms of the general ethos of the class, are significant. Recently, I read a large number of classroom research projects by teachers and was struck by the number of times they mentioned the importance of this aspect of their research. It must be added, however, that pupils need to be introduced to the idea carefully and incrementally. Sudden and radical changes in classroom norms, even if they are for wholly admirable and democratic purposes, can be threatening to pupils unless they have been prepared for it (Rudduck 1984, 1991).

Although these forms of collaboration are very important, they are only illustrative. There are many other forms of professional development that have a bearing on teacher research. Curriculum development, the acquisition of a repertoire of teaching strategies and school/classroom approaches to staff development, are all fundamentally related to classroom research. In the following sections, we look at each of them in turn.

CURRICULUM

Most centralized school systems prescribe what is to be taught to pupils, but require the teacher to put the curriculum into practice. At a very basic level, this involves the teacher in some form of 'translation' of the curriculum policy into schemes of work or lesson plans. More emphasis on research-based teaching would, I believe, result in better 'translations' of centralized curriculum into practice and in teachers who are more confident, flexible and autonomous.

In Chapter 5, I made reference to a Stenhouse suggestion that classroom research be used as a means of testing curriculum ideas. The context of that proposal is worth reproducing in full (Stenhouse 1975: 142–3):

> I have argued that educational ideas expressed in books are not easily taken into possession by teachers, whereas the expression of ideas as curricular specifications exposes them to testing by teachers and hence establishes an equality of discourse between the proposer and those who assess his proposal. There is, of course, no implication as to the origins of the proposal or hypotheses being tested. The originator may be a classroom teacher, a policy-maker or an educational research worker. The crucial point is that the proposal is not to be regarded as an unqualified recommendation but rather as a provisional specification claiming no more than to be worth putting to the test of practice. Such proposals claim to be intelligent rather than correct.
>
> I have identified a curriculum as a particular form of specification about the practice of teaching and not as a package of materials of a syllabus of ground to be covered. It is a way of translating any educational idea into a hypothesis testable in practice. It invites critical testing rather than acceptance.
>
> I have reached towards a research design based upon these ideas, implying that a curriculum is a means of

studying the problems and effects of implementing any defined line of teaching.

The uniqueness of each classroom setting implies that any proposal – even at school level – needs to be tested and verified and adapted by each teacher in his own classroom. The ideal is that the curricular specification should feed a teacher's personal research and development programme through which he is progressively increasing his understanding of his own work and hence bettering his teaching.

To summarize the implications of this position, all well-founded curriculum research and development, whether the work of an individual teacher, of a school, or of a group working in a teachers' centre or of a group working within the co-ordinating framework of a national project, is based on the study of classrooms. It thus rests on the work of teachers.

Here Stenhouse is linking classroom research by teachers firmly to the curriculum and teaching. This is an important point that may have been lost in all the talk about the gathering and analysis of data. Teacher research is not an end in itself, but is inextricably linked to curriculum change and the adoption of new teaching strategies. It is a vehicle for curriculum reform and development.

Times have changed since Stenhouse wrote this and the obvious question that now arises is, 'Can this approach to curriculum development work within the context of a National Curriculum?' My immediate response is to say that a National Curriculum makes this approach all the more necessary. There are also a number of strategies for involving teachers in the implementation of the National Curriculum, such as the one proposed by Denis Lawton (1989: 90–93) in the following extract:

The Practical Task of Implementing the National Curriculum at School Level

It may be useful to analyse stage by stage, what a school

staff would need to do in order to implement the national curriculum.

Stage 1 – Aims

There is a danger that schools will be tempted simply to accept the national curriculum in the form of a list of subjects, assessment tasks and programmes of study, and try to put them directly into operation. This would be to ignore the point that it is necessary to go back at least one stage before converting objectives into teaching programmes.

The first task for a school staff to undertake will be to discuss the aims of the school. This is essential, but dangerous – it could take years to reach complete agreement. It will be better to impose a time limit on this discussion, work towards as much consensus as possible, and list disagreements for resolution (if possible) at later stages.

Teachers will certainly want to look at the DES list of aims, for example those contained in *Better Schools* (DES 1985):

1 To help pupils to develop lively, enquiring minds, the ability to question and argue rationally and to apply themselves to tasks, and physical skills.
2 To help pupils to acquire understanding, knowledge and skills relevant to adult life and employment in a fast-changing world.
3 To help pupils to use language and number effectively.
4 To help pupils to develop personal moral values, respect for religious values, and tolerance of other races, religions and ways of life.
5 To help pupils to understand the world in which they live, and the inter-dependence of individuals, groups and nations.
6 To help pupils to appreciate human achievements and aspirations.

Teachers are likely to come to the conclusion that these aims are generally acceptable but not sufficiently specific for detailed curriculum planning.

Stage 2 – Cultural analysis: core and foundation subjects
The next stage will be to look at the proposed list of subjects for the national curriculum (core and foundation) and discuss their adequacy for a delivery system for the aims referred to above. This could involve the kind of cultural analysis employed in Chapter 3 of Lawton's (1989) book *Education, Culture and the National Curriculum*. The discussion should lead naturally to the adequacy of the ten subjects as a method of *delivering* the desired curriculum. This stage will include looking at 'programmes of study' provided by subject working groups to see what is included and how they can best be converted into teaching and learning schemes.

Stage 3 – Identifying gaps
The discussion of the core and foundation subjects listed above will highlight the fact that not all desirable content will emerge automatically from a simple list of subjects. [There is also of course the] cross-curricular work needed to cover such areas as health education. If the staff agree to some extent with my analysis they will add political, economic and moral education to the list of desirable areas to be covered.

Stage 4 – Filling gaps
The teachers then have to decide, given the particular nature of the school, its local environment and catchment area, how best to fill the gaps identified in Stage 3 above. This will be a question of tactics rather than grand strategy but none the less important for that. Some schools which have already gone through

this process found that it was helpful to think in terms of a more flexible timetable.

Stage 5 – The timetable
Having agreed on possible solutions, it will be necessary to put them into operation by means of a revised timetable. Once again, making use of the experiences of other schools will avoid learning the hard way.

Stage 6 – Evaluation
It will be essential to give teachers an opportunity to discuss progress, and if necessary to make changes.

This, of course, is not the only way of involving teachers in the implementation of the National Curriculum. The National Curriculum Council (1990), for example, have suggested a similar approach in their document on *The Whole Curriculum*. Whatever approach is adopted, the important point is that the process will be greatly enhanced if the teachers involved in this work go about it in the spirit of classroom research.

TEACHING

It seems to me that, in the UK, it is often the case that teaching strategies take second place to curriculum content. This is unfortunate for at least two reasons. First, in a situation where curricula are being increasingly imposed by central authorities, there is still the opportunity for teachers to be selective in the use of teaching strategies. Secondly, it is now evident that the content of a lesson notwithstanding, the use of appropriate teaching strategies can dramatically increase student achievement (Joyce and Showers 1988). A major goal for school improvement, therefore, is for teachers who are so professionally flexible that they can select, from a repertoire of models, the teaching approach most suited to a particular content area and their students' age and ability (Joyce *et al.* 1992). Equally, a major focus for classroom research should be the teaching–learning process. There are at least three aspects of teaching that classroom researchers could focus on: research on teaching effects, the acquisition of a repertoire of 'models of teaching' and the 'artistry' of teaching.

There is an extensive research literature on *teaching effects*. Consistently high levels of correlation are achieved between student achievement scores and classroom processes (see Brophy and Good 1986). This is very complex territory, the intricacies of which are beyond the scope of this chapter. One general conclusion, however, stands out: 'The most consistently replicated findings link achievement to the quantity and pacing of instruction' (Brophy and Good 1986: 360). It is naive to assume that the amount of time spent teaching is in itself a sufficient condition for student achievement. The literature on teaching effects is replete with the cues and tactics necessary for effective teaching. Doyle (1987: 95), as we have already seen, provides a useful summary:

> Classroom studies of teaching effects have generally supported a direct and structured approach to instruction. That is, students usually achieve more when a teacher:
>
> • Emphasizes academic goals, makes them explicit, and expects students to be able to master the curriculum;
> • Carefully organizes and sequences curriculum experiences;
> • Clearly explains and illustrates what students are to learn;
> • Frequently asks direct and specific questions to monitor students' progress and check their understanding;
> • Provides students with ample opportunity to practice, gives prompts and feedback to ensure success,

corrects mistakes, and allows students to practice a skill until it is overlearned or automatic;
- Reviews regularly and holds students accountable for work.

From this perspective, a teacher promotes student learning by being *active* in planning and organizing his or her teaching, explaining to students what they are to learn, arranging occasions for guided practice, monitoring progress, providing feedback, and otherwise helping students understand and accomplish work. Although this list may appear commonsensical, it is still worth 'putting to the test of practice' through the use of classroom research procedures.

But teaching is not just about short-term tactical responses. It is also about the consistent and strategic use of various *teaching models* (Joyce *et al.* 1992). There is a strong body of research to suggest that student achievement is enhanced by the use of particular and specific teaching approaches. Based on their pioneering research and using the concept of effect size, Bruce Joyce and his colleagues (Joyce *et al.* 1987: 13) claim that:

> Research conducted in the last ten years yields impressive evidence for the effectiveness of a variety of innovative teaching practices:
>
> - *Cooperative learning* approaches, representing social models of teaching, yield effect sizes from modest to high. The more complex the outcomes – higher-order thinking, problem solving, social skills and attitudes – the greater are the effects.
> - *Information-processing* models, especially the use of advance organizers and mnemonics, yield modest to substantial effect sizes; and the effects are long-lasting.
> - *Synectics and non-directive teaching* increase student creativity and enhance self concept as well as

effecting student achievement in such basic areas as recall of information.

- *DISTAR*, an example of the *behavioural* family of models, yields modest effect sizes in achievement and, further, influences aptitude to learn.
- When these models and strategies are combined, they have even greater potential for improving student learning.

There is another aspect of teaching which is of great importance to the lay person as well as the classroom research community; this is the impact of a *teachers' 'artistry'* or personality on the individual student. The teacher 'who made a difference' is a common topic of conversation following one's admission that 'I am a teacher'. As Lou Rubin (1985: v) comments in his book *Artistry in Teaching*:

> There is a striking quality to fine classrooms. Students are caught up in learning; excitement abounds; and playfulness and seriousness blend easily because the purposes are clear, the goals sensible, and an unmistakable feeling of well-being prevails.
>
> Artist teachers achieve these qualities by knowing both their subject matter and their students; by guiding the learning with deft control – a control that itself is born out of perception, intuition, and creative impulse.

Can there be any better aspiration for the teacher-researcher? The personality and flair of the individual teacher is increasingly receiving belated attention. For example, one of John Gray's (1990) three performance indicators of an 'effective' school is the proportion of pupils who 'have a good or "vital" relationship with one or more teachers'. This good or vital relationship is a fundamentally important aspect of the teaching process and one that should be at the heart of teacher-based classroom research.

STAFF DEVELOPMENT

We have not as yet built an infrastructure for staff development within our schools. Such an infrastructure would
involve portions of the school week being devoted to staff
development activities, such as curriculum development
and implementation, new models of teaching, regular
observation sessions and on-site coaching. Integral to these
activities is a commitment to reviewing one's performance
as a prelude to development. It is within this context that
classroom research is a fundamental staff development
activity.

Bruce Joyce and Beverly Showers' (1988) work on staff
development, in particular their peer coaching strategy, has
in recent years transformed our thinking on staff development. It is here that there is the closest link with classroom
research techniques, especially observation. Joyce and
Showers identified a number of key training components
which, when used in combination, have much greater
power than when used alone. The major components of
training are:

- presentation of theory or description of skill or strategy,
- modelling or demonstration of skills or models of
  teaching,
- practice in simulated and classroom settings,
- structured and open-ended feedback (provision of information about performance), and
- coaching for application (hands-on, in-classroom assistance with the transfer of skills and strategies to the
  classroom).

Based on this analysis, Joyce and Showers (1984: 85) summarized the 'best knowledge' we have on staff development
like this:

- the use of the integrated theory–demonstration–practice-
  feedback training programme to ensure skill development,

- the use of considerable amounts of practice in simulated conditions to ensure fluid control of the new skills,
- the employment of regular on-site coaching to facilitate vertical transfer, and
- the preparation of teachers who can provide one another with the needed coaching.

More recently, Joyce (1992) has distinguished – helpfully in my opinion – between the two key elements of staff development: the workshop and the workplace. The *workshop*, which is equivalent to the best practice on the traditional INSET course, is where we gain *understanding*, see *demonstrations* of the teaching strategy we may wish to acquire, and have the opportunity to *practise* them in a non-threatening environment. If, however, we wish to transfer these skills that the workshop has introduced us to back into the *workplace* – the classroom and school – then merely attending the workshop is insufficient. The research evidence is very clear that skill acquisition and the ability to transfer vertically to a range of situations requires 'on-the-job support'. This implies changes to the workplace and the way in which we organize staff development in our schools. In particular, this means the opportunity for *immediate and sustained practice, collaboration and peer coaching*, and *studying development and implementation*. We cannot achieve these changes in the workplace without, in most cases, drastic alterations to the ways in which we organize our schools. Yet we will not be able to transfer teaching skills from INSET sessions to a range of classrooms without them. Fortunately, at least for teacher-researchers, as seen in the examples scattered throughout this book, the workplace conditions they create for themselves mesh with and are similar to the core activities of classroom research.

I have tried in these past few pages to demonstrate that classroom research is at the root of key professional development activities such as curriculum development, acquiring a repertoire of teaching strategies and staff development. I have also argued that because of the recent changes, teachers now, more than ever, need to apply the ethic of teacher research to these areas of professional development. The discussion in this chapter has largely centred on how the action can be maintained through teacher development activities; we turn in the following chapter to the broader canvas of school development and explore its links to teacher research.

FURTHER READING

The maintaining of collaborative action has assumed a number of different facets in this chapter. The whole area of reporting research and publication was quite extensively discussed and the main sources were cited. In addition, the various collections of case studies referred to elsewhere in the book provide examples of different ways and styles of reporting. The texts by Rob Walker (*Doing Research*, 1985), Judith Bell (*Doing Your Research Project*, Second Edition, 1993), Jean McNiff (*Action Research*, 1988) and Colin Hook (*Studying Classrooms*, 1981) provide further advice. The links between teacher research and curriculum are obviously central to the work of Lawrence Stenhouse, which has been extensively referred to. Malcolm Skilbeck's (1984) *School Based Curriculum Development* and more recent writing on the implementation of the National Curriculum such as Denis Lawton's (1989) *Education, Culture and the National Curriculum*, extend the arguments contained in this chapter. Teaching tends in my opinion to be a neglected area: exceptions are Chris Kyriacou's *Effective Teaching in Schools* (1986) and *Essential Teaching Skills* (1991). More American in style but central to the arguments contained in this chapter are the practical and comprehensive *Models of Teaching* by Bruce Joyce and his colleagues (1992) and Good and Brophy's (1984) *Looking in Classrooms*. The key text on staff development for our purposes is Joyce and Showers' (1988) *Student Achievement Through Staff Development*.

Other helpful advice on staff development and INSET are Howard Bradley's (1991) *Staff Development*, Wideen and Andrews' (1987) *Staff Development for School Improvement* and the books by Bolam (1982), Easen (1985), Hewton (1988), Lomax (1990), McBride (1989) and O'Sullivan and his colleagues (1988).

> ## CHAPTER 11

Classroom Research and School Improvement

Over the past ten years or so, the amount of change expected of teachers and schools has increased enormously. As well as the curriculum and organizational changes with which we are all too familiar, there are also a number of central policy initiatives in England and Wales that are potentially supportive of teacher and school development. Whether by accident or design, changes in the funding and delivery of staff development, schemes for school self-evaluation, the introduction of teacher appraisal and school development planning are all supportive of what David Hargreaves (1994) has called the 'new professionalism'. We should also note that these recent innovations are 'content free'. Although most have a carefully specified process, the substance or focus of each is for the teacher and the school to decide. Taken together, all of these activities can combine or 'braid' together to form an 'infrastructure' at the school level to support the management of change and the professional development of teachers.

Looking across all of these 'developmental changes', a major common denominator is classroom research. Classroom observation in particular is a fundamental strategy for evaluation, appraisal, development planning, as well as curriculum development and the acquisition of new teaching strategies. Our experience on the DES funded 'School Teacher Appraisal' and 'School Development Plans' projects, as well as our other school improvement work at the Institute of Education in Cambridge, convinces me of the crucial role classroom observation and research can play in supporting the professional growth of teachers and the process of school development.

In this chapter, I will briefly discuss ways in which classroom observation and research can support teacher and school development, with particular reference to school self-evaluation, curriculum evaluation, teacher appraisal and school development planning. As space precludes a complete description of each of these strategies, I will concentrate on the classroom research related skills involved in each of these approaches. I conclude the chapter by briefly discussing how these various activities can combine to create a school-based approach to educational change that supports the achievement of students and the work of teachers.

SCHOOL SELF-EVALUATION

Perhaps the most obvious and longstanding link with classroom research has been the relationship with school self-evaluation. Teacher research and school self-evaluation can be regarded as the two sides of the same coin. They both provide the means whereby teachers and schools can obtain a degree of autonomy within the educational system. Classroom research emancipates (to use Stenhouse's word) teachers from authoritative forms of knowledge, theory and policy; and school self-evaluation – and more recently school development planning – enable a

school to take more control of its curriculum and organization and plan its future more effectively and independently. Both activities also share a common set of
procedures, which relate to a self-conscious and systematic
attempt to review what they (both as individuals and
organizations) are doing and to proceed to action based on
that analysis.

Local education authority (LEA) schemes for school
self-evaluation or school-based review became very popular
in the early to mid-1980s. By the middle of 1982, for
example, four-fifths of the LEAs in England and Wales had
devised schemes for systematic school-based review. These
schemes had one major feature in common: virtually all
included a booklet of classified questions or statements
about schools and schooling.

Perhaps the best known of the schemes for school
self-evaluation was 'GRIDS', which began as a Schools
Council project based at the University of Bristol. The focus
of GRIDS is the internal development of schools. GRIDS
was designed to help teachers to review and develop the
curriculum and organization of their school, and two
practical handbooks – one primary, one secondary – were
produced for the purpose (McMahon *et al.* 1984). In its
second stage, GRIDS was modified in order to recognize the
need to be externally accountable, widen the roles of those
who contribute to a review, assist with the identification of
in-service needs and the management of change. New
materials were also developed to assist teachers in establishing criteria for effectiveness and in using GRIDS in
secondary schools at the department level (Abbott *et al.*
1988).

The aims of GRIDS can best be judged from this extract
from the *GRIDS School Handbook* (McMahon *et al.* 1984):

> The materials in this handbook are designed to help
> teachers review and develop their curriculum and
> organisation. The title 'GRIDS' or 'guidelines for
> review and internal development in schools' has been

carefully chosen. First, the materials are *guidelines*: they contain structured step-by-step advice about how to conduct a school review and development exercise; schools are not expected to follow these suggestions slavishly but rather to adapt and amend them as required. Second, the focus is on *review* leading to *development* for improvement and not on something that stops short at the review stage. Third, the word *internal* indicates that the review is not for external accountability purposes. Finally, the word *school* emphasises that the GRIDS process is directed at the whole school rather than at individual teachers or small groups.

The central practical recommendation in the GRIDS method is that the staff should not attempt to make a detailed review of all aspects of the school at once. Instead, they should take a broad look at what is happening in the school, on the basis of this identify one or two areas that they consider to be priorities for specific review and development, tackle these first, evaluate what they have achieved, and then select another priority. The process has been broken down into a series of key steps and tasks which have a logical structure, and a systematic step-by-step approach is recommended throughout. The five stages in this cyclical problem-solving process are outlined in Fig. 11.1.

Stage 1, *getting started*, is where preliminary decisions have to be made about whether or not the GRIDS method would be appropriate for the school and, if so, how it should be managed. The purpose of stage 2, the *initial review*, is to identify the topics that the staff consider to be priorities for specific review and development. Stage 3 is a *specific review* of the topic(s) that have been identified as priorities; it entails a careful examination of current practice and an assessment of its effectiveness before making recommendations about development. Stage 4 is the *action stage*, when the recommendations are put into practice. Stage 5,

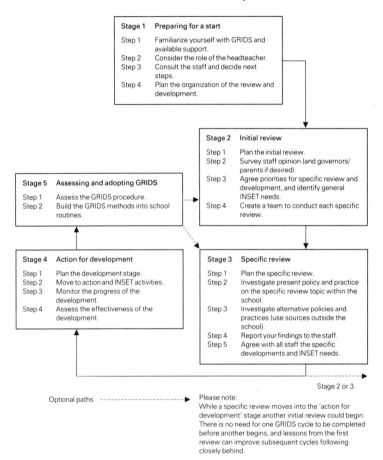

Stage 1   Preparing for a start

Step 1   Familiarize yourself with GRIDS and available support.
Step 2   Consider the role of the headteacher.
Step 3   Consult the staff and decide next steps.
Step 4   Plan the organization of the review and development.

Stage 2   Initial review

Step 1   Plan the initial review.
Step 2   Survey staff opinion (and governors/parents if desired).
Step 3   Agree priorities for specific review and development, and identify general INSET needs.
Step 4   Create a team to conduct each specific review.

Stage 5   Assessing and adopting GRIDS

Step 1   Assess the GRIDS procedure.
Step 2   Build the GRIDS methods into school routines.

Stage 4   Action for development

Step 1   Plan the development stage.
Step 2   Move to action and INSET activities.
Step 3   Monitor the progress of the development.
Step 4   Assess the effectiveness of the development.

Stage 3   Specific review

Step 1   Plan the specific review.
Step 2   Investigate present policy and practice on the specific review topic within the school.
Step 3   Investigate alternative policies and practices (use sources outside the school).
Step 4   Report your findings to the staff.
Step 5   Agree with all staff the specific developments and INSET needs.

Stage 2 or 3

Optional paths ------------------➤

Please note:
While a specific review moves into the 'action for development' stage another initial review could begin. There is no need for one GRIDS cycle to be completed before another begins, and lessons from the first review can improve subsequent cycles following closely behind.

Fig. 11.1 The GRIDS cycle. Reproduced with the permission of SCDC Publications.

overview and restart, is where evaluation of the development work and of the whole process takes place, and a new cycle of review and development begins.

Our current work suggests that schools find carrying out a full review of all provision and practice very time-consuming. In the past, schemes of school-based review demanded a thorough examination of the life and work of the school and two or three terms were often set aside for this. Development work for subsequent years was then planned on the basis of this review. Today, the pressure for change makes this approach less appropriate. We suggest that this energy is now best used in carrying out a series of small-scale focused or specific 'audits' in key areas and in implementing the action plans that may result from these enquiries. A planned series of specific audits creates a rolling programme which provides a picture of the school built up over successive years.

The other problem identified from the evaluation of GRIDS was an apparent lack of rigour and objectivity in many review and development procedures. It appears, unsurprisingly, that school self-evaluation requires that teachers be trained for it. The links here with classroom research are obvious. If the staff involved in GRIDS and similar evaluations had been experienced in classroom research, not only would the reviews have been more 'reliable', but closer links would have been established between the whole school evaluation and classroom practice. This point applies not only to school self-evaluation but also to curriculum evaluation in general, as we see in the following section.

CURRICULUM EVALUATION

There has been a great increase in curriculum evaluation in the UK in recent years. The proliferation of 'categorically funded' curriculum projects such as TVEI, centrally initiated curriculum and assessment innovations such as records of achievement, and a plethora of other government legislation tend to have an evaluation brief attached to them. Although many of these evaluations were initially 'externally funded', increasingly much of this evaluation activity has become school-based. Unfortunately, this approach to evaluation, instead of building on the traditions of classroom research, has remained wedded to an academic view of evaluation that is based on the ubiquitous evaluation report. Most evaluation reports have a notoriously short half-life, and even their limited usefulness is often squandered through bureaucratic delays and an unsuitable style of presentation. This creates particular problems for those of us committed to a developmental approach to evaluation.

This point is particularly poignant in the current climate of change in the UK where many of the recent developments are contentious. Evaluation, which has an improvement perspective, provides a structure for teachers and others to subject a particular curriculum change to their own professional judgement and, in so doing, to improve the programme and make further plans for implementation. In this way, an evaluation can provide a means for translating an educational idea into practice as well as monitoring and enhancing curriculum development. This was the central theme of my book *Evaluation for School Development* (Hopkins 1989), where I tried to outline an approach to evaluation that:

- built on the best practice of classroom research in so far as it supported development and was linked to classroom practice,
- was sufficiently pragmatic to serve the decision-making purposes of evaluation, and
- as far as possible fitted into the day-to-day life of the school.

One of the approaches to school-focused evaluation described in the book was based around the use of the evaluation question. In some evaluations the questions are obvious and immediate, in others they emerge as part of the evaluation. Evaluation questions can be very helpful in focusing your research, and can emerge in a number of ways:

- from the evaluation contract or brief,
- from one's own or the evaluation team's initial planning, and
- after preliminary investigation of the area of evaluation.

1 A linear approach

| Take a specific evaluation issue | 'To what extent is TAC awareness shared by all staff in the establishment?' |

| Derive evaluation questions that can be used | 'Does Technology feature in the Schemes of Work in all subjects?' 'What definitions of Technology are used by Heads of Department?' 'What is the students' experience of Technology in other core subjects?' |

| Choose an appropriate evaluation methodology | This might include, respectively: document search; interview; student questionnaire. |

2 An evolutionary approach

| Take a broad area for investigation | Gender issues in the provision of TAC |

| Carry out initial investigation and analyse data | Analysis of enrolment data and exam results. Classroom observation of some Technology lessons. Unstructured interviews with teachers/students. |

| Derive evaluation questions that can be used | 'Why did more boys than girls enrol for this course this year?' 'Are the practical activities appropriate or interesting to girls?' |

| Choose an appropriate evaluation methodology | This might include, respectively: student interview; structured observation and interview. |

Fig. 11.2 Formulating evaluation questions.

Two approaches to the formulation of questions in an evaluation of 'Technology Across the Curriculum' (TAC) follow as worked examples (see Fig. 11.2).

An evaluation question is, simply, a question that can be answered by some form of structured investigation or research. In this context, it is important to:

- Avoid grandiose questions outside the scope of formative evaluation, such as: 'Is TVEI Extension a "Good Thing"?'
- Avoid long-term questions outside the time-frame: 'Are this year's students getting a better experience of Technology?'
- Avoid questions that are only answerable by large-scale or very technical research.
- Aim for suitably defined questions that can be addressed through the limited quantity of data you can be expected to collect.

Although the formulation of evaluation questions is often quite challenging, this should not deter us from asking tough 'bottom line' questions that reflect the various stages in the change process. Obviously, not all the following questions will apply to every evaluation, but the following examples are the types of questions that will help us assess the impact of a curriculum change on student achievement and the process of school improvement.

- What changes have occurred in teachers' or students' knowledge base?
- What changes have occurred in teachers' or students' skill level and use?
- What changes have occurred in teachers' or students' opinions and feelings?
- What changes have occurred in the culture or organization of the school?
- What changes have occurred in student tests or examinations?

This general approach to evaluation includes four major activities:

1 *Agree on evaluation questions.* Generating questions helps focus the evaluation. Often the questions will relate to the school development plan priorities. It is important not to be too ambitious about the number and scope of the questions asked.

2 *Determine information needs and collection methods.* Once the questions are generated, clarified and prioritized, some way of answering them has to be devised. Potential information sources and collection methods should be identified for each evaluation question. The more sources and methods used, the greater the likelihood that the information will be valid. One way of structuring this important stage in the design of the evaluation is to use a simple worksheet as outlined in Fig. 11.3. As you begin to formulate your evaluation question(s) and devise appropriate data-gathering methods, it

Question	Source	Collection method	Responsibility	Time-line
How was the plan for the delivery of TAC formulated? Was the process effective?	TAC co-ord; school co-ord	Interviews	Evaluator	Oct.–Dec.
What is the plan? Why was this method of delivery chosen?	TAC/school co-ord's; staff	Review documents; questionn-aires; interviews	TAC co-ord; evaluator	Jan.–Mar.
Have students received 10% balanced TAC? Does the reality reflect the plan?	Staff; students	Interviews; Questionn-aires	Co-ordinator; evaluator	Easter onward

Fig. 11.3 A practical evaluation schedule.

is helpful to 'cost' them in terms of: (1) the time it will take to complete the work and (2) the time and people available to you. The plan shown in Fig. 11.3 is an example of an evaluation schedule for Technology Across the Curriculum.

3 *Collect and analyse information.* This activity should co-exist with data collection. Early checks allow evaluators to seek new information sources if necessary and to identify emerging and unanticipated outcomes.

4 *Reports.* Feedback should normally occur as soon as possible, and be tailored to its audience and include follow-up activities if required. This may include reporting to governors and parents and providing information for the school's next development plan. The reports need not be written; they may be given orally with handouts containing summaries of data as 'back-up' material. Often, reduced data are sufficient to act as a basis for discussion. When reports are written they should be short; often data summaries can be prepared on one side of A4. They should also distinguish clearly between the presentation of data and any interpretation that may be made of the results.

An overview of this evaluation process is given in Fig. 11.4. This figure is of course too linear and, in reality, a number of these steps co-exist and time-lines tend to merge. It may also be that questions have to be refined and unanticipated logistical problems may occur during the evaluation. An obvious precaution is to ensure that time-lines are realistic, that one is not expecting too much too soon, and that as many problems as possible are anticipated.

Two further points need to be made about this process. The first is that there needs to be a logic or flow between the evaluation question, the data collected, analysis, feedback and the resulting action. In that way, the evaluation develops a power of its own because each stage builds on the other. The second is to make certain that the evaluation questions are important to the school and staff concerned. Evaluation is so time-consuming that its results should not

Fig. 11.4 The evaluation process.

be gratuitous, but feed real need and be able to provide useful and pertinent information.

The most usual data sources for evaluations of this type are observations, interviews, questionnaires and documents.

Observations (e.g. of staff meetings) will involve the evaluator in observing the planning process in a variety of real-life contexts. Before you start, you will need to decide how to record your observations and to have some idea of the processes you hope to observe. As a great deal will be happening, it is important to have a clear focus before you begin, but be flexible and note down unexpected outcomes as well.

Interviews will tend to be focused on the evaluation questions. The responses can normally be recorded manually on an interview form. As the questions will usually be about issues and events familiar to both the interviewer and interviewee, it is important to avoid predetermining their responses. It is suggested that you elicit their general view of the situation before asking more specific questions.

Questionnaires of the standardized variety are not usually part of an evaluation exercise like this. If it is felt that a questionnaire will provide useful information, then you could use a short open-ended series of questions. This could be on one or two pages of A4 with 4–6 pertinent questions.

Finally, a survey of *documentary evidence* (e.g. policy statements, curriculum materials) provides an important first step in getting to know about the school and LEA. Another important source of documentary data are diaries kept by those involved in the planning process and/or a series of memos produced by the investigator. Both diaries and memos will contain a rich source of subjective evidence and the potential for verbatim quotations in the case study report. Needless to say, the use of these sources in an evaluation is determined by the most appropriate source of data for a particular evaluation question.

Analysing one's data is also extremely important. The methods described in Chapter 9 apply equally here. There are a number of ways of checking that your understanding about the situation is valid. For example:

- check opinions of what has happened from the points of view of several groups or individuals,
- use multiple (at least two) data collection methods, so that the results from each can be compared,
- establish clear links between the evidence and what you report,
- check relevant sections of your report with those involved,
- check for alternative explanations about what might have happened,

- be clear and rigorous over the analysis of the data you collect.

The important point is to ensure that another evaluator would come to the same conclusions as yourself given the same material. Although more focused than traditional classroom research, this evaluation approach builds on the good practice of teacher-researchers.

TEACHER APPRAISAL

Another recent major central government initiative that has potentially strong links with classroom research is teacher appraisal. Despite the bad press that appraisal has received in some quarters, it does offer teachers excellent opportunities for professional development. Our evaluation of the 'School Teacher Appraisal Pilot Study' (Bradley *et al.* 1989) gives strong evidence that a professional development model of appraisal can work. Our interviews with hundreds of teachers up and down the country give striking examples of the enthusiasm and professional growth that appraisal can generate if the process is carefully managed. The cycle of activities associated with appraisal is relatively well known and is illustrated in Fig. 11.5. The most obvious link between appraisal and classroom research is in the 'data collection' phase (see Fig. 11.6), especially classroom observation.

During the evaluation of the 'School Teacher Appraisal Pilot Study', we saw a number of advantages of classroom observation. In particular, it:

- offers teachers feedback on their teaching,
- offers teachers an 'extra pair of eyes', i.e. a chance to find out more about what is happening in their classroom,
- encourages collaboration between colleagues and the exchange of ideas,
- encourages more reflection about teaching,
- encourages better lesson preparation,

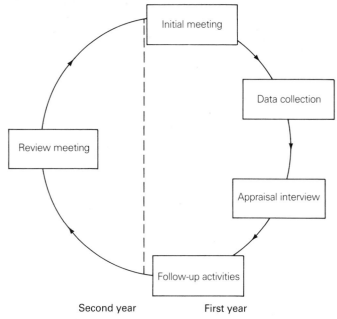

Fig. 11.5 The elements of appraisal (from Bradley 1992: 34).

- ensures that an appraisal interview is based on knowledge of a teacher's real work,
- can lead to focusing on common issues across a school or department and enable subsequent follow-up by the group involved,
- breaks down classroom isolation, and
- provides support.

Classroom observation is, of course, likely to be a sensitive experience for teachers unused to regular or systematic observation since their early days in the profession. It is, however, something which can be valuable in its own right and used for other staff and curriculum development purposes besides appraisal. Experience suggests that initial apprehension disappears once the process of observation is under way, providing appropriate procedures are used. Experience also suggests the many applications of observation skills become clearer in the course of

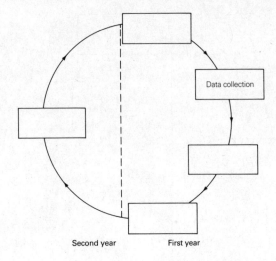

Second year   First year

- Self-appraisal
    the individual's perspective
    blank sheet or prompt list?
    sharing?
- Classroom observation
    focused
    jointly planned
    feedback
    observation skills
    establishing criteria
- Task observation
- Interviews and questionnaires
    establish code of practice
- Other available information
    schemes of work
    pupils' work.

Fig. 11.6 Teacher appraisal: Data collection (from Bradley 1992: 2–3).

the appraisal process. For example, observation skills developed during appraisal can be used when observing pupils as part of National Curriculum assessment.

Classroom observation appears to work best if:

1 It is set in a cycle of:

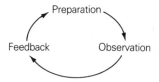

2 At the preparation stage, the observer and teacher meet:
- to agree the time/place of the observation,
- to agree the focus and method,
- to agree the time for feedback,
- to agree on the style of the observation (e.g. participant or not),
- to discuss the context of the lesson and any constraints, and
- to agree the criteria to be used in discussing the lesson.
3 It is on selected areas of classroom life. Some restriction of what is looked at is likely to lead to better quality observation and more factual feedback.

I have already discussed in Chapter 6 some of the main principles of classroom observation, and it may be useful to briefly describe here some training activities we have used to promote good practice.

The first activity is designed to acquaint participants with the three-phase cycle of classroom observation. The activity utilizes video examples (possibly taken from the excellent series of videos made by those LEAs involved in the appraisal pilot) to provide 'action images' which participants can relate to their own experience. The session could be divided into five parts:

1 *Overview of benefits of the three-phase cycle.*
2 *Video example of the planning meeting.* In discussing the video, participants may wish to consider:
- How important is negotiation in the whole process?
- What skills are involved?

- What is the relationship between the participants?
- How realistic is the agreed focus?

3 *Video example of the classroom observation*. During the video, participants should be encouraged to keep in mind the agreed focus of the observation and make notes on it as if they were in the classroom. In discussing the video, participants may wish to consider:

- What other areas of focus could have been identified?
- How feasible was it to obtain information on the agreed focus?
- What skills were needed by the observer?
- What are the relative benefits of open or focussed observation?

4 *Video example of the feedback discussion*. In discussing the video, participants may wish to consider:

- How far do you agree with the points raised in the discussion?
- What is the balance between judgement and reflection in the discussion?
- How far can this discussion lay the basis for professional growth?
- What skills are required by an observer in promoting the developmental nature of such a discussion?

5 *Review the classroom observation process in relation to the five key issues discussed earlier.*

The second activity is designed to aid thinking about which areas to focus on in classroom observation and suitable data collection methods. Each group member should in turn select an aspect of their work as a possible focus for classroom observation and outline it to the group. The remainder of the group should then discuss:

- What information could be gathered through classroom observation?
- How would the observer collect it?
- How would the observer record it?
- What are the criteria that could most helpfully be applied to this particular aspect of the teacher's work?

Area of focus	Information needs	How to collect	How to record	Criteria

As each member of the group presents an example and the others respond to it, the group should build up an *aide-mémoire* using the table above. The *aide-mémoire* may then be helpful in designing appropriate observation instruments or schedules and for identifying the most appropriate criteria to inform the feedback discussion.

If possible, back in school, participants should ask a colleague to use the approach devised during this exercise in their classroom and then to report back to other colleagues on how well it worked. Our experience during the appraisal pilot emphasized the usefulness of 'dry runs' like this in acquiring the skills of, and allaying fears about, classroom observation.

In this section, I have emphasized the role of classroom observation in teacher appraisal. Obviously, there is more to appraisal than this, but it is here where the links between classroom research are the closest. We have found in many schools that as the process of classroom observation for appraisal gathers pace, many other applications of observation skills become clear. When they are linked to other whole school initiatives, classroom observation and appraisal become increasingly powerful tools for professional development and are regarded as generic staff development activities. Our school improvement experience suggests that when initiatives are linked together in this way, they become a powerful means for achieving whole school development. Many of these links can be established through the use of the school's development plan, which we turn to in the following section.

SCHOOL DEVELOPMENT PLANNING

Our experience on the DES 'School Development Plans' project suggests that development planning provides a means of linking together a variety of initiatives, which in turn can build on the traditions of classroom research. As the DES booklet *Planning for School Development* (Hargreaves *et al.* 1989) noted, the distinctive feature of a *development plan* is that it brings together, in an overall plan, national and LEA policies and initiatives, the school's aims and values, its existing achievements and its needs for development. By co-ordinating aspects of planning which are otherwise separate, the school acquires a shared sense of direction and is able to control and manage the tasks of development and change. Priorities for development are planned in detail for one year and are supported by action plans or working documents for staff. The priorities for later years are sketched in outline to provide the longer-term programme.

There is no space in this chapter to review development planning in any detail, but Fig. 11.7 provides an overview of the whole process. Those interested in the wider issues should consult our book, *The Empowered School* (Hargreaves and Hopkins 1991). In this section, I will concentrate on the somewhat neglected area of action planning, because once again this provides the closest links to teacher research and classroom practice. (The following discussion is based on more detailed descriptions in the *The Empowered School* (Hargreaves and Hopkins 1991), and the DES booklet *Planning for School Development* (Hargreaves *et al.* 1989) to which the interested reader should turn for more information.)

Once the development plan is agreed, the chosen prior-

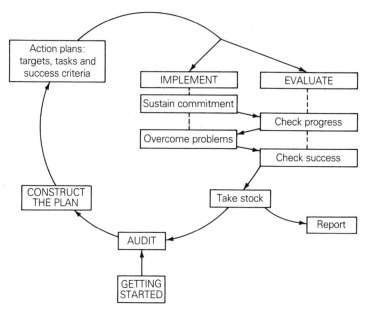

Fig. 11.7 The planning process (reproduced with permission from Hargreaves and Hopkins 1991: 66).

ities have to be turned into more detailed *action plans*. These are the working documents for teachers. Priorities are subdivided into targets, which specify the tasks involved and who will be responsible for them. The targets and tasks establish what is to be done. The success criteria establish the basis for judging whether the targets have been met.

Each *action plan* describes, preferably on one side of A4, the programme of work to be undertaken. It contains:

- the *priority* as described in the development plan,
- the *targets* or the more specific objectives for the priority,
- the *success criteria* against which progress and success in reaching targets can be judged,
- the *tasks* or work to be undertaken to reach each target (these may be attached as an appendix): there are tasks for both implementation and evaluation,

- the *allocation of responsibility* for targets and tasks, with time-lines,
- the dates for meetings *to assess progress*, and
- the *resource* implications (materials and equipment, finance, INSET, etc.).

The action plan is therefore a convenient summary of and guide to action. An example of an action plan, in this case on home–school links in a primary school, is given in Fig. 11.8.

In our work on development planning, we treat the

Priority: to improve our partnership with parents and to devise a home–school reading scheme.

Target 1: survey of parents' views during first term.

Success criteria: (i) number of parents responding; (ii) quality of the response to each of the three main issues in the survey (details to be decided after questions are framed).

Target 2: write policy for home–school reading, inform parents of it through newsletter and review book stock, also in first term if possible.

Success criteria: (i) adviser to judge quality of policy; (ii) judgement of parent-governors and reaction of parents to newsletter; (iii) review of stock to be defined during the activity.

Target 3: involvement of parents in the workshops and book fair and in the home–school reading scheme; publication of articles in local newspaper (second or third term, depending on progress).

Success criteria: (i) attendance of parents and their response to the workshops and book fair; (ii) changes in parental behaviour judged by borrowing of books and pupils' reports on home reading; (iii) changes in pupil attitudes to reading judged by observation and increase in reading skills; (iv) more community involvement in reading judged by comments of staff and parent-governors.

Time: three terms

Dates: for progress checks – by all at each meeting
for success checks – by Mrs Green as appropriate

Resources: for new book stock and newsletter

Co-ordinator: Mrs Green

Fig. 11.8 Action plan for home–school partnership (reproduced with permission from Hargreaves and Hopkins 1991: 57).

processes of implementation and evaluation as interlaced, not as a period of implementation followed by a 'big bang' evaluation at the end. If implementation and evaluation are linked, evaluation can help to shape and guide the action plan rather than being a *post mortem* upon it. The key to the integration of implementation and evaluation is the action plan. When the targets and success criteria are clear and specific, implementation and evaluation become easier.

Teachers often find defining the success criteria the most difficult part of the action plan. It is much easier to break down a priority into targets and tasks than it is to define success criteria. Targets must, however, specify the criteria by which success in reaching the target can be judged, both by team members and by others. These *success criteria* are a form of school-generated performance indicator, which:

- give *clarity* about the target: what exactly are you trying to achieve?
- point to the *standard* expected by the team,
- provide advance warning of the *evidence* needed to judge successful implementation, and
- give an indication of the *time-scale* involved.

The success criteria are a means of evaluating the outcomes of the plan, as well as providing benchmarks for development. It is important that they specify the minimal acceptable standard, though the team will usually have aspirations to a standard of outcome which is much higher than this.

There are a number of examples of success criteria in Fig. 11.8. Some of them are quantitative (e.g. number of parents responding) and some qualitative (e.g. quality of response to each of the three main issues . . .). In the latter case, the exact details of the criteria have to be decided at a later date, after the questions have been framed; so that becomes a task in itself. With one of the other qualitative success criteria, someone external to the school (in this case an adviser) is asked to help judge quality. In all of these cases, the use of evidence is mentioned in the action plan, and the *aide-mémoire* of tasks contains both implementation and evaluation activities.

At least once a term, progress should be formally checked for each task against the success criteria associated with the target. The team will need some clear *evidence* of the extent of progress: if such evidence is recorded, the workload at a later stage will be reduced.

A *progress check* is an act of evaluation, *in the course of* implementation. It is a response to the question, 'How are we doing so far?' Many progress checks are intuitive, a 'feel' for whether things are going well or badly. This is a natural part of monitoring one's activities: it becomes more systematic if these intuitive reactions are shared within the team, and evidence is produced to support them. Regular progress checks involve:

- giving somebody in the team responsibility for ensuring that the progress checks take place,
- reviewing progress at team meetings, especially when taking the next step forward or making decisions about future directions,
- deciding what will count as evidence of progress in relation to the success criteria,
- finding quick methods of collecting evidence from different sources, and
- recording the evidence and conclusions for later use.

Success checks take place at the end of the developmental work on a target. The team now decides how successful the implementation of the target or priority as a whole has been. Checking success need not be complex or time-consuming. It will consist largely in collating, and then drawing a conclusion about, the earlier progress checks.

To summarize, once the action plan is being implemented, the evaluation tasks are monitored through the *progress* and *success* checks. Prior to implementation, however, it is helpful to have some form of *readiness check* to ensure that the basic requirements for action are in place.

Development planning, therefore, requires teachers to use their professional judgement in a systematic way to evaluate progress, and it is here where classroom research skills are most needed. Teachers already, monitor and evaluate their own actions as well as the behaviour and work of pupils, as part of their everyday activities. Using *intuitive* and *considered* (i.e. checking where necessary the basis of an intuitive judgement) professional judgements is a routine part of being a teacher. Both are a natural and inherent part of evaluating progress and success in the implementation of a development plan.

Nowadays, however, innovations often create new working circumstances with which the teacher is less familiar. In these instances, professional judgements may be less trustworthy than usual. If so, a *refined professional judgement* is required. This is an opportunity for enhancing professional judgement, and is achieved:

- through discussion with colleagues about the extent of progress or success in implementing a priority,
- by establishing agreement on standards used to make judgements,
- through mutual observation in the classroom, and
- through the use of informed opinion.

In short, development planning provides ample opportunities for teachers to talk with others, to seek agreement on standards, to observe one another and to read relevant documentation: all are means of refining the professional judgements which are essential to evaluation.

There are circumstances when teachers need to *complement* even a refined professional judgement with additional evidence collected through classroom research procedures. This would include when others need to be persuaded of the validity of teachers' judgements, or when there are benefits to all, if the teachers' judgements are backed by independent evidence.

The basis for evaluating how far targets and success criteria are met will often consist of a mixture of professional judgements and complementary evidence. Collecting complementary evidence is usually more time-consuming than making professional judgements, so careful thought needs to be given to questions such as: What kind of complementary evidence is appropriate to documenting success? How can it be collected as quickly and easily as possible without adding substantially to existing workloads?

Extending teachers' professional judgements through action planning therefore links the professional development of the individual teacher to the development of the school as a whole as well as improving the quality of teaching and learning.

SCHOOL IMPROVEMENT

The days when schools had to contend with single innovations are long gone. These are times of innovation overload, when multiple changes have to be managed simultaneously, and we have to learn new strategies to cope with constant and complex change. In our experience, the essential strategy consists in selecting areas for action, in finding connections between these areas, and in ensuring that there is an adequate infrastructure to support the strategy. This infrastructure is composed of the links between strategies such as staff development, evaluation, appraisal and planning on the one hand, and the classroom research and similar skills of the teaching staff on the other. Our more successful schools exploit innovation, they take the opportunity of the recent changes and use them to support developments already underway or planned for in the school. In short, they adapt external change for internal purpose.

A couple of examples will illustrate the point. First, the science department in a large secondary school had put teaching strategies to support their schemes of work for KS 3 (which had been the focus of their previous year's development work) on the current year's development plan. With the introduction of appraisal, they took the opportunity to use some of the time devoted to classroom observation, together with time already allocated from the staff development budget, to observe each other teach. They based their observations on the criteria 'for good science teaching at KS 3' they had jointly developed in previous staff development sessions. They used their regular meeting time for discussion of the observations, and to plan further collaborative enquiry on the teaching strategies and schemes of work.

Second, during the evaluation of the 'School Teacher Appraisal Pilot Study' in Cumbria, we found that the GRIDS approach to school self-evaluation was used not only to create a suitable context and climate for the introduction of teacher appraisal, but also as a means of enhancing the work of a school. Particularly in primary schools, GRIDS both provided a useful context for teacher appraisal and resulted in significant specific curriculum developments. Involvement in this whole school exercise encouraged staff to talk collectively about and analyse their practice, and it created a coherent focus for development work which provided a backdrop for individual appraisal. What the teachers were actually doing, however, was 'reflective enquiry' or classroom research within a whole school context.

These schools successfully balanced school and individual needs, and in so doing altered the ways in which staff worked together. If changes such as these are to be more than just 'bolt-on-extras', then some changes also have to be made to aspects of the school's organization or management arrangements. This approach to educational change, which is known as school improvement, is concerned with school process as well as student outcomes. School improvement is about enhancing the teaching–learning process and the conditions which support it. School improvement emphasizes the importance of the culture and organization of the school as key factors in sustaining teacher and curriculum development. So those who work in the field of school improvement actively seek to enhance student outcomes through specific changes in teaching approaches and the curriculum, and through strengthening the school's organizational ability to support the work of teachers. As I hope has become apparent in the last two chapters, teacher-researchers have a key role to play in these developments.

FURTHER READING

This chapter has touched on a broad range of issues that has a vast supporting literature. What follows is therefore inevitably selective. In terms of curriculum evaluation, McCormick and James' (1988) *Curriculum Evaluation in Schools* has already been mentioned, as well as my own *Evaluation for School Development* (Hopkins 1989). The OU reader *Evaluating Education* (Murphy and Torrance 1987) is a helpful source, as is Kath Aspinall and colleagues' (1992) *Managing Evaluation in Education*. As regards school self-evaluation, the GRIDS handbooks (McMahon *et al.* 1984; Abbott *et al.* 1988) are essential reading. Of interest also is Phil Clift and colleagues' (1987) *Studies in School Self Evaluation*, as well as our own work on school-based review (Bollen and Hopkins 1987; Hopkins 1988). Teacher appraisal now has an extensive literature, so I will be excused for being a little partisan! Our involvement at the Institute of Education in Cambridge in the 'Evaluation of the School Teacher Appraisal Pilot Study' has resulted in (among other publications) *An Introduction to Teacher Appraisal* (Bollington *et al.* 1990), *Training for Appraisal: A Set of Distance Learning Materials* (Bollington and Bradley 1990), the *Report on the Evaluation of the School Teacher Appraisal Pilot Study* (Bradley *et al.* 1989) and West and Bollington's (1990) *Teacher Appraisal: A Practical Guide for Schools*. In addition, good background information to appraisal in England and Wales is to be found in *Teacher Appraisal: A Nationwide Approach* (Evans and Tomlinson 1989). Our work on development planning resulted in the DES booklet *Planning for School Development* (Hargreaves *et al.* 1989) and *The Empowered School* (Hargreaves and Hopkins 1991). There are now a number of practical guides to planning of which Mel West and Mel Ainscow's (1991) *Managing School Development* is the best. Finally, the literature on school improvement is also growing. Comprehensive treatments are found in *The Structure of School Improvement* (Joyce *et al.* 1983), *Alternative Perspectives on School Improvement* (Hopkins and Wideen 1984), *Improving the Quality of Schooling* (Hopkins 1987), *Innovation and Change* (Rudduck 1991) and *Successful School Improvement* (Fullan 1992). We have reported our own school improvement work in 'Aboard the moving school' (Ainscow and Hopkins 1992) and *School Improvement in an Era of Change* (Hopkins *et al.* 1994). Last but by no means least, the standard text on educational change is Michael Fullan's (1991) *The New Meaning of Educational Change*.

▷ **CHAPTER 12**

Seeing Teacher Development Whole

In his evocative essay *The Tree*, John Fowles (1979) talks of the importance of 'seeing nature whole'. He argues against the contemporary reductionist and utilitarian view of the environment which alienates us from the source of nature itself. By fragmenting nature, by categorizing it, by breaking it up into little pieces so that we can 'understand it', we lose its essence. The more we try to control nature in this way, the more we move away from and fail to grasp its vital spirit. So it is with teacher development. The more we regard teachers as functionaries, the more we move towards reductionist notions of 'competency' and dull the spark of creative artistry, the more we improverish the teaching and learning in our schools.

Much has changed in education in the eight years between writing the first and second editions of this book. Not all the change has in my opinion been for the best. I am particularly concerned that many of the changes have come at the expense of teacher development. One of the ways of restoring the balance, I believe, is to re-emphasize the role of the teacher-researcher and firmly locate this role within a whole school context. I want in these final pages to expand a little on this theme and argue for seeing teacher and school development 'whole'.

The past ten years, in particular, have seen a plethora of comprehensive changes. There have been in many countries seemingly contradictory pressures for centralization (i.e. increasing government control over policy and direction) on the one hand, and de-centralization (i.e more responsibility for implementation, resource management and evaluation at the school level) on the other. At the same time as the national government has drawn to itself more power than ever before, the usual infrastructure of support has been eroded and schools are finding themselves increasingly alone in the struggle to take charge of the process of change. All of this has placed enormous pressures on teachers and schools.

As we move into the 1990s, the educational agenda will be increasingly dominated by a concern to implement the centralized educational reforms of the 1980s. As a result, attention will begin to focus on the achieving of a functional school-centred system, on the competence and development of teachers and school leaders, and on school cultures that promote and sustain quality. This quest for stability will, however, continue to be sought against a background of continuing change, as rising expectations of student achievement are frequently accompanied by radical changes in the way schools are governed and managed. What price quality and reflection in such turbulent times?

Paradoxically, much of the recent legislation is having the unintended consequence of eroding the traditional culture of individualism in teaching by forcing structural changes that are generating new forms of collaboration. David Hargreaves (1994) has, as we have already noted, called this change in the values and practices of teachers a 'new professionalism'. In a somewhat perverse way, the new changes are perhaps unwittingly creating the conditions and structures to make this possible. Hargreaves (1994) describes the new professionalism in relation to nine themes which, because they are occurring concurrently, present an almost irresistible pressure for change. Somewhat ironically, they also provide fertile ground for professional development.

Among these nine themes is the move from 'individualism to collaboration'. As we have already seen, in order to implement the National Curriculum successfully, teachers are forced to create new forms of collaboration if they do not already exist. The changes in teacher education are also forcing a move from 'supervision to mentoring', which presupposes a more explicit professional and reflective role on the part of the individual mentor-teacher, and an inevitable shift in social relations through the developing of new professional partnerships in schools which have a number of mentors and students. The shift from 'hierarchies to teams' is another example seen in many secondary schools which reflects imaginative responses to the cross-curricular demands of the National Curriculum.

These are only three examples of this trend towards the 'new professionalism'. The important point in this context is that once again the skills and aptitudes of the teacher-researcher are well suited to this new professional role. At the same time, the activities presupposed by the new professionalism provide an ideal vehicle for 'maintaining the action' of teacher research. These links with teacher classroom research are fundamental. Indeed, those schools that are successfully managing the change process and at the same time enhancing the quality of education for their students, are full of teachers who, if not actively practising classroom research, are *au fait* with its philosophy and approach.

In making his argument, Hargreaves sets out two propositions about the relationship between teacher and school development. The first is that *there is little school development without teacher development*. The second is that *there is little teacher development without school development*. The truth of the first proposition is axiomatic. This book and virtually every citation in it is based on that premise. The second proposition is more controversial; but it is at the heart of the difference between this book and the one I wrote eight years ago. Put simply, then I believed that to improve schools we needed to improve teachers, to build a community of teacher-researchers. Now I believe that to sustain the ethic of teacher development we need to anchor our work to a whole school context.

Happily, I am finding that those schools where something akin to Hargreaves' 'new professionalism' is emerging, also tend to be those that are successfully coping with the national reform agenda. They are doing this (albeit in many cases intuitively) by finding practical ways of bringing together teacher and school development. This synthesis is both a contributor to, and a product of, the new professionalism.

But as I have implied already, it increasingly seems to me that teacher research alone is not enough. Reflective classroom practice needs to be linked to whole school development. We are currently working with some forty schools on our Improving the Quality of Education for All (IQEA) project (see Ainscow and Hopkins 1992; Hopkins *et al.* 1994). Many of these schools are using the development plan as an overarching strategy that focuses innovative efforts on a limited number of priorities, generates ownership and galvanizes support. The priorities tend to relate to teaching and classroom organization in a broad sense, rather than curriculum in the conventional sense. Many of our schools are using some form of classroom or 'paired' observation to help staff work together and to learn from each other. The effectiveness of this approach is considerably enhanced when the observation is underpinned by an agreed specification of the teaching strategy to be employed. This provides a 'standard' for the mutual observation, a detailed outline of the nature of the developmental activity, as well as a language for talking about teaching. Indeed, peer observation is proving to be a powerful means for establishing ownership, of acquiring new teaching strategies and eventually transforming the culture of the school.

This and the other examples scattered throughout the book suggest that what are needed are powerful and integrative implementation strategies that directly address the nature of teaching and the culture of the school. Our current work with these schools suggests that it is through linking more precise specifications of teaching to classroom research strategies within the context of the development plan that progress is made. Strategies for school improvement that do not link teaching to whole school activities are 'doomed to tinkering'. In short, we need to see teacher and school development whole. When we do this we not only begin to meet the real challenge of educational reform, but we also create classrooms and schools where both our children and their teachers learn.

Ethics for Classroom Research

Action researchers must pay attention to the ethical principles guiding their work. Their actions are deeply embedded in an existing social organization and the failure to work within the general procedures of that organization may not only jeopardize the process of improvement but existing valuable work. Principles of procedure for action research accordingly go beyond the usual concerns for confidentiality and respect for the persons who are the subjects of enquiry and define in addition, appropriate ways of working with other participants in the social organization. The principles outlined below reflect the commitment implicit in the methods of action research to participation and collaborative work, and negotiation within, and ultimately beyond existing social and political circumstances.

Observe protocol: Take care to ensure that the relevant persons, committees and authorities have been consulted, informed and that the necessary permission and approval has been obtained.

Involve participants: Encourage others who have a stake in the improvement you envisage to shape the form of the work.

Negotiate with those affected: Not everyone will want to be directly involved; your work should take account of the responsibilities and wishes of others.

Report progess: Keep the work visible and remain open to suggestions so that unforeseen and unseen ramifications can be taken account of; colleagues must have the opportunity to lodge a protest to you.

Obtain explicit authorization before you observe: For the purposes of recording the activities of professional colleagues or others (the observation of your own students falls outside this imperative provided that your aim is the improvement of teaching and learning).

Obtain explicit authorization before you examine files, correspondence or other documentation: Take copies only if specific authority to do this is obtained.

Negotiate descriptions of people's work: Always allow those described to challenge your accounts on the grounds of fairness, relevance and accuracy.

Negotiate accounts of others' points of view (e.g., in accounts of communication): Always allow those involved in interviews, meetings and written exchanges to require amendments which enhance fairness, relevance and accuracy.

Obtain explicit authorization before using quotations: Verbatim transcripts, attributed observations, excerpts of audio and video recordings, judgements, conclusions or recommendations in reports (written or to meetings).

Negotiate reports for various levels of release: Remember that different audiences demand different kinds of reports; what is appropriate for an informal verbal report to a faculty meeting may not be appropriate for a staff meeting, a report to council, a journal article, a newspaper, a newsletter to parents; be conservative if you cannot control distribution.

Accept responsibility for maintaining confidentiality.

Retain the right to report your work: Provided that those involved are satisfied with the fairness, accuracy and relevance of accounts which pertain to them; and that the accounts do not unnecessarily expose or embarrass those involved; then accounts should not be subject to veto or be sheltered by prohibitions of confidentiality.

Make your principles of procedure binding and known: All of the people involved in your action research project must agree to the principles before the work begins; others must be aware of their rights in the process.

Reprinted, with permission, from the *Action Research Planner* (Kemmis and McTaggart, 1981: 43–44).

▷ References

Abbott, R., Birchenough, M. and Steadman, S. (1988) *GRIDS School Handbooks*, 2nd edn (Primary and Secondary versions). York: Longman for the SCDC.

Acheson, K. and Gall, M. (1980) *Techniques in the Clinical Supervision of Teachers*. New York: Longman.

Adelman, C. (1981) *Uttering, Muttering*. London: Grant McIntyre.

Ainscow, M. and Hopkins, D. (1992) 'Aboard the moving school'. *Educational Leadership*, 50(3), 79–81.

Armstrong, M. (1980) *Closely Observed Children*. London: Writers and Readers.

Armstrong, M. (1982) 'The story of five stories: An enquiry into children's narrative thought'. Unpublished mimeo.

Aspinall, K., Simkins, T., Wilkinson, J. and McAuley, J. (1992) *Managing Evaluation in Education*. London: Routledge.

Barrow, R. (1986) 'Research into teaching, the conceptual factors'. *Educational Research*, 28(3), 220–30.

Becker, H. (1958) 'Problems of inference and proof in participant observation'. *American Sociological Review*, 28, 652–60 (reprinted in McCormick, 1982, op cit.).

Bell, J. (1993) *Doing Your Research Project* (Second Edition). Milton Keynes: Open University Press.

Bolam, R. (1982) *School-Focussed In-Service Training*. London: Heinemann.

Bollen, R. and Hopkins, D. (1987) *School Based Review: Towards a Praxis*. Leuven: ACCO.

Bollington, R. and Bradley, H. (1990) *Training for Appraisal: A Set of Distance Learning Materials*. Cambridge: CIE.

Bollington, R., Hopkins, D. and West, M. (1990) *An Introduction to Teacher Appraisal*. London: Cassell.

Bolster, A. (1983) 'Towards a more effective model of research on teaching'. *Harvard Educational Review*, 53(3), 294–308.

Bowen, B., Forsyth, K., Green, J. *et al.* (undated) *Ways of Doing Research in One's Own Classroom*. Cambridge: Cambridge Institute of Education, Ford Teaching Project.

Bradley, H. (1991) *Staff Development*. Lewes: Falmer Press.

Bradley, H. (1992) *Ready for Appraisal*, 2nd edn. Cambridge: CIE.

Bradley, H., Bollington, R., Dadds, M. *et al.* (1989) *Report on the Evaluation of the School Teacher Appraisal Pilot Study*. Cambridge: CIE.

Brophy, J. (1981) 'Teacher praise: A functional analysis'. *Review of Educational Research*. 51, 5–32.

Brophy, J. and Good, T. (1986) 'Teacher behaviour and student achievement'. In Wittrock, M. (ed.) *Handbook of Research on Teaching*, 3rd edn. New York: Macmillan.

Campbell, D. and Stanley, J. (1963) 'Experimental and quasi-experimental designs for research on teaching'. In Gage, N. (ed.) *Handbook of Research on Teaching*. Chicago: Rand McNally.

Carr, W. (ed.) (1989) *Quality in Teaching*. Lewes: Falmer Press.

Carr, W. and Klemmis, S. (1986) *Becoming Critical*. Lewes: Falmer Press.

Clift, P., Nuttal, D. and McCormick, R. (1987) *Studies in School Self Evaluation*. Lewes: Falmer Press.

Cogan, M. (1973) *Clinical Supervision*. Boston, MA: Houghton Mifflin.

Congdon, P. (1978) 'Basic principles of sociometry'. *Association of Education Psychologists Journal*, 4(8), 5–9.

Corey, S. (1953) *Action Research to Improve School Practice*. New York: Teacher's College Press.

Croll, P. (1986) *Systematic Classroom Observation*. Lewes: Falmer Press.

Cronbach, L. (1975) 'Beyond the two disciplines of scientific psychology'. *American Psychologist*, 30(2), 116–27.

Deakin University (1982) *The Action Research Reader*. Victoria: Deakin University Press.

Delamont, S. (1983) *Interaction in the Classroom*. London: Methuen.

Delamont, S. (1984) *Readings on Interaction in the Classroom*. London: Methuen.

Delamont, S. (1992) *Fieldwork in Educational Settings*. Lewes: Falmer Press.

Department of Education and Science (1985) *Better Schools*. London: HMSO.

Dillon, J. (1983) 'Problem solving and findings'. *Journal of Creative Behaviour*, 16(2), 97–111.

Doyle, W. (1987) 'Research on teaching effects as a resource for improving instruction'. In Wideen, M. and Andrews, I. (eds) *Staff Development for School Improvement*. Lewes: Falmer Press.

Dunn, W. and Swierczek, F. (1977) 'Planned organizational change: Toward grounded theory'. *Journal of Applied Behavioural Science*, 13(2), 135–57.

Easen, P. (1985) *Making School-centred INSET Work*. London: Croom Helm.

Ebbutt, D. (1985) 'Educational action research: Some general concerns and specific quibbles'. In Burgess, R. (ed.) *Issues in Educational Research*. Lewes: Falmer Press.

Ebbutt, D. and Elliott, J. (eds) (1985) *Issues in Teaching for Understanding*. York: Longman.

Elbaz, F. (1983) *Teacher Thinking – A Study of Practical Knowledge*. London: Croom Helm.

Elliott, J. (1976) *Developing Hypotheses about Classrooms from Teachers' Practical Constructs*. Cambridge: Cambridge Institute of Education, Ford Teaching Project.

Elliott, J. (1981) 'Action research: Framework for self-evaluation in schools'. TIQL Working Paper No. 1. Cambridge: Cambridge Institute of Education, mimeo.

Elliott, J. (1991) *Action Research for Educational Change*. Milton Keynes: Open University Press.

Elliott, J. and Adelman, C. (1976) *Innovation at the Classroom Level: A Case Study of the Ford Teaching Project*. Unit 28, Open University Course E 203: Curriculum Design and Development. Milton Keynes: Open University Educational Enterprises.

Elliott, J. and Ebbutt, D. (1985a) *Facilitating Educational Action Research in Schools*. York: Longman.

Elliott, J. and Ebbutt, D. (eds) (1985b) *Case Studies in Teaching for Understanding*. Cambridge: Cambridge Institute of Education.

Evans, A. and Tomlinson, J. (1989) *Teacher Appraisal: A Nationwide Approach*. London: Jessica Kingsley.

Fisher, R. (1935) *The Design of Experiments*. Edinburgh: Oliver and Boyd.

Flanders, N. (1970) *Analysing Teaching Behaviour*. Reading, MA: Addison-Wesley.

Fowles, J. (1979) *The Tree*. St Albans: Sumach Press.

Fullan, M. (1991) *The New Meaning of Educational Change*. London: Cassell.

Fullan, M. (1992) *Successful School Improvement*. Buckingham: Open University Press.

Gage, N. (1978) *The Scientific Basis of the Art of Teaching*. New York: Teachers College Press.

Galton, M. (1978) *British Mirrors*. Leicester: University of Leicester School of Education.

Galton, M., Simon, B. and Croll, P. (1980) *Inside the Primary Classroom*. London: Routledge and Kegan Paul.

Gambrell, L. (1981) 'Extending think-time for better reading instruction'. *Education Digest*, February, pp. 33–5.

Gibson, R. (1986) *Critical Theory and Education*. London: Hodder and Stoughton.

Glaser, B. and Strauss, A. (1967) *The Discovery of Grounded Theory*. New York: Aldine.

Goldhammer, R., Anderson, R. and Krajewski, R. (1980) *Clinical Supervision: Special Methods for the Supervision of Teachers*, 2nd edn. New York: Holt, Rinehart and Winston.

Good, T. and Brophy, J. (1984) *Looking in Classrooms*, 3rd edn. New York: Harper and Row.

Gray, J. (1990) 'The quality of schooling: Frameworks for judgement'. *British Journal of Educational Studies*, 38(3), 203–223.

Hamilton, D., Macdonald, B., King, C. *et al.* (eds) (1977) *Beyond the Numbers Game*. Berkeley, CA: McCutchan.

Hammersley, M. (ed.) (1986) *Controversies in Classroom Research*. Milton Keynes: Open University Press.

Hammersley, M. and Atkinson, P. (1983) *Ethnography: Principles in Practice*. London: Tavistock.

Hargreaves, D. H. (1994) 'The new professionalism: A synthesis of professional and institutional development. *Teaching and Teacher Education*, 10(4).

Hargreaves, D. H. and Hopkins, D. (1991) *The Empowered School*. London: Cassell.

Hargreaves, D. H., Hopkins, D., Leask, M. *et al.* (1989) *Planning for School Development*. London: DES.

Hewton, E. (1988) *School Focused Staff Development*. Lewes: Falmer Press.

Hitchcock, G. and Hughes, D. (1989) *Research and the Teacher*. London: Routledge.

Hook, C. (1981) *Studying Classrooms*. Victoria: Deakin University Press.

Hopkins, D. (1982) 'Doing research in your own classroom'. *Phi Delta Kappan*, 64(4), 274–5.

Hopkins, D. (1984a) 'Teacher research: Back to the basics'. *Classroom Action Research Network Bulletin*, No. 6, pp. 94–9.

Hopkins, D. (1984b) 'Towards a methodology for teacher based classroom research'. *School Organization*, 4(3), 197–204.

Hopkins, D. (1987) *Improving the Quality of Schooling*. Lewes: Falmer Press.

Hopkins, D. (1988) *Doing School Based Review*. Leuven: ACCO.

Hopkins, D. (1989) *Evaluation for School Development*. Milton Keynes: Open University Press.

Hopkins, D., Ainscow, M. and West, M. (1994) *School Improvement in an Era of Change*. London: Cassell.

Hopkins, D. and Reid, K. (eds) (1985) *Rethinking Teacher Education*. London: Croom Helm.

Hopkins, D. and Wideen, M. (eds) (1984) *Alternative Perspectives on School Improvement*. Lewes: Falmer Press.

Hopkins, D., Bollington, R. and Hewett, D. (1989) 'Growing up with qualitative research and evaluation'. *Evaluation and Research in Education*, 3(2), 61–80.

Hull, C., Rudduck, J. and Sigsworth, A. (1985) *A Room Full of Children Thinking*. York, Longman.

Hustler, D., Cassidy, T. and Cuff, T. (eds) (1986) *Action Research in Classrooms and Schools*. London: Allen and Unwin.

Joyce, B. (1992) 'Cooperative learning and staff development research: teaching the method with method?' *Cooperative Learning* Vol 12 No. 2, Winter, pp. 10–13.

Joyce, B. and Showers, B. (1984) 'Transfer of training: The contribution of coaching'. In Hopkins, D. and Wideen, M. (eds) *Alternative Perspectives on School Improvement*. Lewes: Falmer Press.

Joyce, B. and Showers, B. (1988) *Student Achievement Through Staff Development*. New York: Longman.

Joyce, B., Hersh, R. and McKibbin (1983) *The Structure of School Improvement*. New York: Longman.

Joyce, B., Showers, B. and Rolheiser-Bennett, C. (1987) 'Staff development and student learning: A synthesis of research on models of teaching'. *Education Leadership*, 47(2), 11–23.

Joyce, B., Weil, M. and Showers, B. (1992) *Models of Teaching*, 4th edn. Englewood Cliffs, NJ: Prentice-Hall.

Kemmis, S. (1982) 'Action research in retrospect and prospect'. In Deakin University. *The Action Research Reader*. Victoria: Deakin University Press.

Kemmis, S. (1983) 'Action research'. In Husen, T. and Postlethwaite, T. (eds) *International Encyclopedia of Education: Research and Studies*. Oxford: Pergamon.

Kemmis, S. and McTaggart, R. (1988) *The Action Research Planner*, 3rd edn. Victoria: Deakin University Press (1st edn, 1981).

Kyriacou, C. (1986) *Effective Teaching in Schools*. Oxford: Blackwell.

Kyriacou, C. (1991) *Essential Teaching Skills*. Oxford: Blackwell.

Lawton, D. (1989) *Education, Culture and the National Curriculum.* London: Hodder and Stoughton.

Lewin, K. (1946) 'Action research and minority problems'. *Journal of Social Issues,* 2, 34–46.

Lincoln, Y. and Guba, E. (1985) *Naturalistic Enquiry.* Beverly Hills, CA: Sage.

Lomax, P. (ed.) (1990) *Managing Staff Development in School.* Clevedon: Multilingual Matters.

Lortie, D. (1975) *School Teacher.* Chicago: University of Chicago Press.

Louis, K. S. and Miles, M. (1990) *Improving the Urban High School.* New York: Teacher's College Press.

MacDonald, B. and Walker, R. (eds) (1974) *Innovation, Evaluation Research and the Problem of Control.* Norwich: CARE, University of East Anglia Press.

Magee, B. (1973) *Popper.* London: Fontana/Collins.

May, N. and Rudduck, J. (1983) *Sex Stereotyping and the Early Years of Schooling.* Norwich: School of Education, University of East Anglia Press.

McBride, R. (ed.) (1989) *The In-Service Training of Teachers.* Lewes: Falmer Press.

McCormick, R. (ed.) (1982) *Calling Education to Account.* London: Heinemann.

McCormick, R. and James, M. (1988) *Curriculum Evaluation in Schools,* 2nd edn. London: Croom Helm.

McKernan, J. (1991) *Curriculum Action Research.* London: Kogan Page.

McMahon, A., Bolam, R., Abbott, R. and Holly, P. (1984) *GRIDS School Handbooks* (Primary and Secondary versions). York: Longman for the Schools Council.

McNiff, J. (1988) *Action Research: Principles and Practice.* London: Macmillan.

Miles, M. and Huberman, M. (1984a) 'Drawing valid meaning from qualitative data: Toward a shared craft'. *Educational Researcher,* 13(5), 20–30.

Miles, M. and Huberman, M. (1984b) *Qualitative Data Analysis: A Sourcebook of New Methods.* Beverly Hills, CA: Sage.

Murphy, R. and Torrance, H. (1987) *Evaluating Education.* London: Harper and Row.

National Curriculum Council (1990) *Curriculum Guidance: The Whole Curriculum.* York: NCC.

Nixon, J. (ed.) (1981) *A Teacher's Guide to Action Research.* London: Grant and McIntyre.

Oja, S. N. and Smulyan, L. (1989) *Collaborative Action Research.* Lewes: Falmer Press.

Open University (1976) *Personality and Learning,* Course E201. Milton Keynes: Open University.

Open University (1980) *Curriculum in Action.* Milton Keynes: LMSO.

O'Sullivan, F., Jones, K. and Reid, K. (1988) *Staff Development in Secondary Schools.* London: Hodder and Stoughton.

Patton, M. Q. (1980) *Qualitative Evaluation Methods.* Beverly Hills, CA: Sage.

Polyani, M. (1962) *Personal Knowledge.* Chicago: University of Chicago Press.

Pring, R. (1978) 'Teacher as researcher'. In Lawton, D., Gordon, P., Ing, M. *et al.* (eds) *Theory and Practice of Curriculum Studies.* London: Routledge and Kegan Paul.

Rapoport, R. (1970) 'Three dilemmas in action research'. *Human Relations,* 23, pp. 1–11.

Rowland, S. (1984) *The Enquiring Classroom: An Introduction to Children's Learning.* Lewes: Falmer Press.

Rubin, L. (1985) *Artistry in Teaching.* New York: Random House.

Rudduck, J. (1981) *Making the Most of the Short Inservice Course.* London: Methuen.

Rudduck, J. (ed.) (1982) *Teachers in Partnership: Four Studies of Inservice Collaboration.* York: Longman.

Rudduck, J. (1984) 'Introducing innovation to pupils'. In Hopkins, D. and Wideen, M. (eds) *Alternative Perspectives on School Improvement.* Lewes: Falmer Press.

Rudduck, J. (1991) *Innovation and Change.* Buckingham: Open University Press.

Rudduck, J. and Hopkins, D. (eds) (1985) *Research as a Basis for Teaching.* London, Heinemann.

Rudduck, J. and Sigsworth, A. (1985) 'Partnership supervision'. In Hopkins, D. and Reid, K. (eds) *Rethinking Teacher Education.* London: Croom Helm.

Sandford, N. (1970) 'Whatever happened to action research?' *Journal of Social Issues,* 26(4), 3–23.

Schon, D. (1983) *The Reflective Practitioner.* New York: Basic Books.

Schwandt, T. and Halpern, E. (1988) *Linking Auditing and Meta Evaluation.* Beverly Hills, CA: Sage.

Simon, A. and Boyer, E. (1975) *Mirrors for Behaviour: An Anthology of Classroom Observation Instruments.* Philadelphia: Research for Better Schools Inc.

Simons, H. (1982) 'Suggestions for a school self evaluation based on democratic principles'. In McCormick, R. (ed.) *Calling Education to Account.* London: Heinemann.

Simons, H. (1987) *Getting to Know Schools in a Democracy.* Lewes: Falmer Press.

Skilbeck, M. (1984) *School Based Curriculum Development*. London: Harper and Row.

Smith, L. and Geoffrey, W. (1968) *The Complexities of an Urban Classroom*. New York: Holt, Rinehart and Wilson.

Stenhouse, L. (1970) *The Humanities Project*. London: Heinemann. Revised edition by Rudduck, J. (1983) Norwich: School of Education, University of East Anglia Press.

Stenhouse, L. (1975) *An Introduction to Curriculum Research and Development*. London: Heinemann.

Stenhouse, L. (1979) 'Using research means doing research'. In Dahl, H., Lysne, A. and Rand, P. (eds) *Spotlight on Educational Research*. Oslo: University Press.

Stenhouse, L. (1980) 'Product or process: A response to Brian Crittenden'. *New Education*, 2(1), 137–40.

Stenhouse, L. (1983) *Authority, Education and Emancipation*. London: Heinemann.

Stenhouse, L. (1984) 'Artistry and teaching: The teacher as focus of research and development'. In Hopkins, D. and Wideen, M. (eds) *Alternative Perspectives on School Improvement*. Lewes: Falmer Press.

Stenhouse, L., Verma, G., Wild, R. and Nixon, J. (1982) *Teaching About Race Relations*. London: Routledge and Kegan Paul.

Strauss, A. (1987) *Qualitative Analysis for Social Scientists*. Cambridge: Cambridge University Press.

Strauss, A. and Corbin, J. (1990) *Basics of Qualitative Research*. Newbury Park, CA: Sage.

Walker, R. (1985) *Doing Research*. London: Methuen.

Walker, R. and Adelman, C. (1975) *A Guide to Classroom Observation*. London: Methuen.

Webb, R. (ed.) (1990) *Practitioner Research in the Primary School*. Lewes: Falmer Press.

West, M. and Ainscow, M. (1991) *Managing School Development*. London: David Fulton.

West, M. and Bollington, R. (1990) *Teacher Appraisal: A Practical Guide for Schools*. London: David Fulton.

Whitman, W. (1855/1959) *Leaves of Grass*. New York: Viking.

Wideen, M. and Andrews, I. (eds) (1987) *Staff Development for School Improvement*. Lewes: Falmer Press.

Winter, R. (1989) *Learning from Experience*. Lewes: Falmer Press.

Young, R. (1989) *A Critical Theory of Education*. Hemel Hempstead: Harvester Wheatsheaf.

▷ Name Index

▷ Subject Index

DOING YOUR RESEARCH PROJECT (2nd edition)
A GUIDE FOR FIRST-TIME RESEARCHERS IN EDUCATION AND
SOCIAL SCIENCE

Judith Bell

If you are a beginner researcher, the problems facing you are much the
same whether you are producing a small project, an MEd dissertation
or a PhD thesis. You will need to select a topic; identify the objectives
of your study; plan and design a suitable methodology; devise
research instruments; negotiate access to institutions, material and
people; collect, analyse and present information; and finally, produce
a well-written report or dissertation. Whatever the scale of the
undertaking, you will have to master techniques and devise a plan of
action which does not attempt more than the limitations of expertise,
time and access permit.

We all learn to do research by actually doing it, but a great deal of time
can be wasted and goodwill dissipated by inadequate preparation.
This book aims to provide you with the tools to do the job, to help you
avoid some of the pitfalls and false trails that can eat into your time, to
establish good research habits, and to take you from the stage of
choosing a topic through to the production of a well-planned,
methodologically sound and well-written final report or dissertation
on schedule.

Doing Your Research Project serves as a source of reference and guide
to good practice for all beginner researchers, whether undergraduate
and postgraduate students or professionals such as teachers or social
workers undertaking investigations in Education and the Social
Sciences. This second edition retains the basic structure of the very
successful first edition whilst incorporating some important new
material.

Contents
*Approaches to educational research – Planning the project – Keeping
records and making notes – Reviewing the literature – Negotiating
access and the problems of inside research – The analysis of
documentary evidence – Designing and administering questionnaires – Planning and conducting interviews – Diaries – Observation Studies – Interpretation and presentation of the evidence –
Postscript – References – Index.*

192 pp   0 335 19094 4 (Paperback)

CONTROVERSIES IN CLASSROOM RESEARCH (2nd edition)

Martyn Hammersley (ed.)

Classroom research has given rise to some major theoretical and methodological controversies across a number of disciplines, including psychology, sociology and linguistics. The growing influence of interpretive and ethnographic perspectives has produced a cross-disciplinary shift away from quantitative analysis towards detailed qualitative investigations of classroom interaction, and there has been considerable debate about the relative merits of these two approaches. However, there have also been arguments among representatives of the new approaches to classroom research, for example over how classroom language is to be analysed, about whether macro or micro explanations are the most appropriate, and about the merits and legitimacy of theoretical and action research.

This second edition of the successful *Controversies in Classroom Research* places new emphasis on examining the pros and cons of the teacher-as-researcher movement. It is an important resource for students of education, psychology, and sociology, for teachers on initial and in-service training courses, and for all those interested in classroom research. A companion volume, *Case Studies in Classroom Research* edited by Martyn Hammersley is also published by Open University Press.

Contents
Part 1: Systematic observation and ethnography – Interaction analysis in informal classrooms – The characteristics and uses of systematic observation – Revisiting classroom research – Revisiting Hamilton and Delamont – Part 2: Studying classroom language – Language in classroom interaction – Scratching the surface: linguistic data in educational research – Talking and teaching – Putting competence into action – Part 3: Macro and micro analysis – Ethnography – Self-contained ethnography or a science of phenomenal forms and inner relations – Whatever happened to symbolic interactionism? Some reflections upon the macro–micro problem in the sociology of education – Part 4: Case study and action research – The conduct of educational case studies – An adversary's account of SAFARI's ethics of case-studty – Bread and dreams or bread and circuses? A critique of 'case study' research in education – The teacher as researcher – Action research in education – On practitioner ethnography – Index.

Contributors
C. Adelman, R. Anderson, P. Atkinson, W. Carr, S. Delamont, A. D. Edwards, V. J. Furlong, D. Hamilton, M. Hammersley, D. Hargreaves, D. Jenkins, S. Kemmis, F. W. Lutz, G. Macleod, D. McIntyre, R. Sharp, W. Sharrock, L. Stenhouse, M. Stubbs and R. Walker.

304 pp   0 335 19040 5 (Paperback)

MAKING SENSE OF TEACHING

Sally Brown and Donald McIntyre

This book helps us to understand better the nature of teaching in schools and, in particular, to understand teaching from the perspective of the people doing it: the teachers. The authors seek to gain access to teachers' professional craft knowledge and to facilitate teachers' own articulation of the ordinary, everyday teaching which they do routinely and spontaneously in classrooms. Their emphasis throughout is on investigating 'good teaching', on what goes well in the classroom. They are also concerned to identify how an understanding of the professional craft knowledge of teachers is particularly important for, and applicable to, the preservice and inservice training of teachers, effective curriculum innovation, and teacher appraisal. They help us to make sense of what goes on in good teaching, and draw out the significant implications for policy and practice.

Contents

144 pp   0 335 15795 5 (Paperback)   0 335 15796 3 (Hardback)

EVALUATION FOR SCHOOL DEVELOPMENT

David Hopkins

Teachers and other educationalists are expected increasingly to carry out evaluations of new initiatives. Teachers are being seconded to perform the evaluation task or are expected to evaluate innovations in their own schools. David Hopkins provides a much-needed guide on how to do evaluation in schools and LEAs.

This is an accessible introduction whose primary focus is on *practice*. The conceptual frameworks used in the book provide guidelines for theory in action, and are extensively illustrated by examples of actual practice. As well as providing an overview of evaluation David Hopkins argues that, to be of any value, school focused evaluation must lead to school improvement.

Contents
Section I: What is evaluation? – Evaluation for school development – Approaches to evaluation – Section II: Methods of working – Designing and doing evaluation – Evaluation methods – Analysing data and enhancing validity – Evaluation roles – Section III: Developmental approaches – Evaluating classrooms, departments and cross-curricular initiatives – Whole-school evaluation – Evaluating INSET – Project evaluation – Section IV: Making an impact – Making evaluation formative – Evaluation and school improvement – Further reading – References – Index.

224 pp   0 335 09240 3 (Paperback)   0 335 09241 1 (Hardback)

Liggen in London in lenten an elles.
Somme serven the kyng and his silver tellen,
In cheker and in chancerye chalengen his dettes
Of wardes and wardmotes, weyves and streyves.
95 And some serven as servantz lordes and ladyes,
And in stede of stuwardes sytten and demen.
Here masse and here matynes and many of here oures
Arn don undevoutlych; drede is at the laste
Lest Crist in consistorie acrose ful manye.   (58–99)

(extracts from the B text in *Piers Plowman in Three
Parallel Texts* ed. Walter Skeat [OUP, 1886])

83 **pleyned** complained 84 **pestilence** plague 85 **leve**
permission 86 **symonye** selling the offices of the church 87
bachelers graduates 88 **cure** responsibility for souls **crounyng**
tonsure 92 **tellen** count 93 **cheker** the court of Exchequer
chalengen demand payment of 94 **wardes** royal wards
wardmotes local meetings **weyves** lost property **streyves** stray
animals 96 **stede** place **demen** judge 98 **don** performed
99 **consistorie** church court (but Christ's court is the last judgement)